Tower Air Fryer

Cookbook For Beginners UK

A variety of Delicious Tower Air Fryer Recipes for You And Your Family, Using European Units of Measurement

Linda R. Grimm

CONTENTS

Introduction

This cookbook has been put together as a simple and understandable guide for you as you explore the use of a slow cooker. It is my goal that you will be able to make some lip-licking, drool-worthy but healthy meals while cooking with as little heat as possible.

I put in the effort to ensure that the ingredients used are very easy to find and the processes very easy to follow.

With this, I wish you a good time making dishes that will create lasting memories for you and your family

The air fryer can replace your oven, microwave, deep fryer, and dehydrator, and evenly cook delicious meals in a fraction of the time (and electricity costs) you're used to. Air frying makes it easy to feed your family healthy, irresistible meals with just five ingredients or less!

An air fryer can also help you succeed on the keto diet. Typically, fried foods are loaded with carbohydrates, so you might assume you have to avoid them altogether when on a keto diet. But when you use the air fryer, you can get the distinct crunch and mouthwatering taste of your fried favorites without the carbs. And you can choose your own low-carb breading! Another benefit to air frying is how much it shortens cooking time. This is especially crucial when you are hungry, short on time, and running low on supplies—a recipe for cheating on your diet. That's why your air fryer will be your best friend throughout your keto journey and help you stay on track, without venturing outside of a small list of ingredients and pantry staples.

Let's get air frying!

How Does the Tower Air fryer Works?

The technology of the Tower Air fryer is very simple. Fried foods get their crunchy texture because hot oil heats foods quickly and evenly on their surface. Oil is an excellent heat conductor, which helps with fast and simultaneous cooking across all ingredients. For decades cooks have used convection ovens to mimic the effects of frying or cooking the whole surface of the food. But the air never circulates quickly enough to achieve that delicious surface crisp we all love in fried foods.

With this mechanism, the air is circulated on high degrees, up to 200° C, to "air fry" any food such as fish, chicken or chips, etc. This technology has changed the whole idea of cooking by reducing the fat up to 80% compared to old-fashioned deep fat frying.

The Tower Air fryer cooking releases the heat through a heating element that cooks the food more healthily and appropriately. There's also an exhaust fan right above the cooking chamber, which provides the food required airflow. This way, food is cooked with constant heated air. This leads to the same heating temperature reaching every single part of the food that is being cooked. So, this is an only grill and the exhaust fan that is helping the Tower Air fryer to boost air at a constantly high speed to cook healthy food with less fat.

The internal pressure increases the temperature that will then be controlled by the exhaust system. Exhaust fan also releases extra filtered air to cook the food in a much healthier way. The Tower Air fryer has no odor at all, and it is absolutely harmless, making it user and environment-friendly.

Benefits of the Tower Air Fryer:

•Healthier, oil-free meals

•It eliminates cooking odors through internal air filters

•Makes cleaning easier due to lack of oil grease

•The Tower Air Fryer can bake, grill, roast and fry providing more options

•A safer method of cooking compared to deep frying with exposed hot oil

•Has the ability to set and leave, as most models and it includes a digital timer

The Tower Air fryer is an all-in-one that allows cooking to be easy and quick. It also leads to a lot of possibilities once you get to know it. Once you learn the basics and become familiar with your Tower Air fryer, you can feel free to experiment and modify the recipes in the way you prefer. You can prepare a vast number of dishes in the Tower Air fryer, and you can adapt your favorite stove-top dish, so it becomes air fryer–friendly. It all boils down to variety and lots of options, right?

Cooking perfect and delicious as well as healthy meals has never been easier. You can see how this recipe collection proves itself.

Cleaning Your Air Fryer

Before cleaning it, first ensure that your air fryer is completely cool and unplugged. To clean the air fryer pan you'll need to:

Remove the air fryer pan from the base. Fill the pan with hot water and dish soap. Let the pan soak with the frying basket inside for 10 minutes.

Clean the basket thoroughly with a sponge or brush.

Remove the fryer basket and scrub the underside and outside walls.

Clean the air fryer pan with a sponge or brush.

Let everything air-dry and return to the air fryer base.

To clean the outside of your air fryer, simply wipe with a damp cloth. Then, be sure all components are in the correct position before beginning your next cooking adventure.

Pantry Staples

Each recipe in this book has five or fewer main ingredients, but also included are some additional kitchen staples to help ensure that the tastes and textures of your meals come out perfect. I've identified six nonperishable pantry staples that you likely already have in your kitchen and that you'll want to have on hand when creating the recipes in this book. These staples are:

- All-purpose flour

- Granulated sugar

- Salt

- Ground black pepper

- Baking powder

- Vanilla extract

These must-haves were chosen for their versatility and frequent use not just in the recipes that follow but also in recipes you may collect online, at family gatherings and parties, and more. In each recipe in this book, you'll find a list of which of these staples you'll also need, so be sure to stock up on anything you may be running low on beforehand.

With this final information in hand, you are truly ready to get cooking. Throughout the following chapters you'll find plenty of delicious, five-ingredient recipes to suit all tastes. Use these recipes as your guide, but always feel free to season intuitively and customize dishes to your liking—just be aware that doing so will change the provided nutritional information.

Bread And Breakfast

Green Egg Quiche

Servings: 4
Cooking Time: 30 Minutes
Ingredients:

- 1 cup broccoli florets
- 2 cups baby spinach
- 2 garlic cloves, minced
- ¼ tsp ground nutmeg
- 1 tbsp olive oil
- Salt and pepper to taste
- 4 eggs
- 2 scallions, chopped
- 1 red onion, chopped
- 1 tbsp sour cream
- ½ cup grated fontina cheese

Directions:

1. Preheat air fryer to 375°F. Combine broccoli, spinach, onion, garlic, nutmeg, olive oil, and salt in a medium bowl, tossing to coat. Arrange the broccoli in a single layer in the parchment-lined frying basket and cook for 5 minutes. Remove and set to the side.
2. Use the same medium bowl to whisk eggs, salt, pepper, scallions, and sour cream. Add the roasted broccoli and ¼ cup fontina cheese until all ingredients are well combined. Pour the mixture into a greased baking dish and top with cheese. Bake in the air fryer for 15-18 minutes until the center is set. Serve and enjoy.

Veggie & Feta Scramble Bowls

Servings: 2
Cooking Time: 25 Minutes
Ingredients:

- 1 russet potato, cubed
- 1 bell pepper, cut into strips
- ½ feta, cubed
- 1 tbsp nutritional yeast
- ½ tsp garlic powder
- ½ tsp onion powder
- ¼ tsp ground turmeric
- 1 tbsp apple cider vinegar

Directions:

1. Preheat air fryer to 400°F. Put in potato cubes and bell pepper strips and Air Fry for 10 minutes. Combine the feta, nutritional yeast, garlic, onion, turmeric, and apple vinegar in a small pan. Fit a trivet in the fryer, lay the pan on top, and Air Fry for 5 more minutes until potatoes are tender and feta cheese cooked. Share potatoes and bell peppers into 2 bowls and top with feta scramble. Serve.

Mini Bacon Egg Quiches

Servings:6
Cooking Time: 30 Minutes
Ingredients:

- 3 eggs
- 2 tbsp heavy cream
- ¼ tsp Dijon mustard
- Salt and pepper to taste
- 3 oz cooked bacon, crumbled
- ¼ cup grated cheddar

Directions:

1. Preheat air fryer to 350ºF. Beat the eggs with salt and pepper in a bowl until fluffy. Stir in heavy cream, mustard, cooked bacon, and cheese. Divide the mixture between 6 greased muffin cups and place them in the frying basket. Bake for 8-10 minutes. Let cool slightly before serving.

Egg And Sausage Crescent Rolls

Servings: 8
Cooking Time: 11 Minutes
Ingredients:

- 5 large eggs
- ¼ teaspoon black pepper
- ¼ teaspoon salt
- 1 tablespoon milk
- ¼ cup shredded cheddar cheese
- One 8-ounce package refrigerated crescent rolls
- 4 tablespoon pesto sauce
- 8 fully cooked breakfast sausage links, defrosted

Directions:

1. Preheat the air fryer to 320°F.
2. In a medium bowl, crack the eggs and whisk with the pepper, salt, and milk. Pour into a frying pan over medium heat and scramble. Just before the eggs are done, turn off the heat and add in the cheese. Continue to cook until the cheese has melted and the eggs are finished (about 5 minutes total). Remove from the heat.
3. Remove the crescent rolls from the package and press them flat onto a clean surface lightly dusted with flour. Add 1½ teaspoons of pesto sauce across the center of each roll. Place equal portions of eggs across all 8 rolls. Then top each roll with a sausage link and roll the dough up tight so it resembles the crescent-roll shape.
4. Lightly spray your air fryer basket with olive oil mist and place the rolls on top. Bake for 6 minutes or until the tops of the rolls are lightly browned.
5. Remove and let cool 3 to 5 minutes before serving.

Canadian Bacon & Cheese Sandwich

Servings: 1

Cooking Time: 30 Minutes

Ingredients:

- 1 English muffin, halved
- 1 egg
- 1 Canadian bacon slice
- 1 slice provolone cheese

Directions:

1. Preheat air fryer to 350°F. Put the muffin, crusty side up, in the frying basket. Place a slice of bacon next to the muffins and Bake for 5 minutes. Flip the bacon and muffins, and lay a slice of provolone cheese on top of the muffins. Beat the egg in a small heatproof bowl.

2. Add the bowl in the frying basket next to the bacon and muffins and Bake for 15 minutes, or until the cheese melts, bacon is crispy and eggs set. Remove the muffin to a plate, layer a slice of bacon, then the egg and top with the second toasted muffin.

White Wheat Walnut Bread

Servings: 8

Cooking Time: 25 Minutes

Ingredients:

- 1 cup lukewarm water (105–115°F)
- 1 packet RapidRise yeast
- 1 tablespoon light brown sugar
- 2 cups whole-grain white wheat flour
- 1 egg, room temperature, beaten with a fork
- 2 teaspoons olive oil
- ½ teaspoon salt
- ½ cup chopped walnuts
- cooking spray

Directions:

1. In a small bowl, mix the water, yeast, and brown sugar.
2. Pour yeast mixture over flour and mix until smooth.
3. Add the egg, olive oil, and salt and beat with a wooden spoon for 2minutes.
4. Stir in chopped walnuts. You will have very thick batter rather than stiff bread dough.
5. Spray air fryer baking pan with cooking spray and pour in batter, smoothing the top.
6. Let batter rise for 15minutes.
7. Preheat air fryer to 360°F.
8. Cook bread for 25 minutes, until toothpick pushed into center comes out with crumbs clinging. Let bread rest for 10minutes before removing from pan.

English Muffin Sandwiches

Servings: 4

Cooking Time: 15 Minutes

Ingredients:

- 4 English muffins
- 8 pepperoni slices
- 4 cheddar cheese slices
- 1 tomato, sliced

Directions:

1. Preheat air fryer to 370°F. Split open the English muffins along the crease. On the bottom half of the muffin, layer 2 slices of pepperoni and one slice of the cheese and tomato. Place the top half of the English muffin to finish the sandwich. Lightly spray with cooking oil. Place the muffin sandwiches in the air fryer. Bake for 8 minutes, flipping once. Let cool slightly before serving.

Thai Turkey Sausage Patties

Servings:4

Cooking Time: 30 Minutes

Ingredients:

- 12 oz turkey sausage
- 1 tsp onion powder
- 1 tsp dried coriander
- ¼ tsp Thai curry paste
- ¼ tsp red pepper flakes
- Salt and pepper to taste

Directions:

1. Preheat air fryer to 350°F. Place the sausage, onion, coriander, curry paste, red flakes, salt, and black pepper in a large bowl and mix well. Form into eight patties. Arrange the patties on the greased frying basket and Air Fry for 10 minutes, flipping once halfway through. Once the patties are cooked, transfer to a plate and serve hot.

Brown Sugar Grapefruit

Servings: 2

Cooking Time: 4 Minutes

Ingredients:

- 1 grapefruit
- 2 to 4 teaspoons brown sugar

Directions:

1. Preheat the air fryer to 400°F.
2. While the air fryer is Preheating, cut the grapefruit in half horizontally (in other words not through the stem or blossom end of the grapefruit). Slice the bottom of the grapefruit to help it sit flat on the counter if necessary. Using a sharp paring knife (serrated is great), cut around the grapefruit between the flesh of the fruit and the peel. Then, cut each segment away from the membrane so that it is sitting freely in the fruit.
3. Sprinkle 1 to 2 teaspoons of brown sugar on each half of the prepared grapefruit. Set up a rack in the air fryer basket (use an air fryer rack or make your own rack with some crumpled up aluminum foil). You don't have to use a rack, but doing so will get the grapefruit closer to the element so that the brown sugar can caramelize a little better. Transfer the grapefruit half to the rack in the air fryer basket. Depending on how big your grapefruit are and what size air fryer you have, you may need to do each half separately to make sure they sit flat.
4. Air-fry at 400°F for 4 minutes.
5. Remove and let it cool for just a minute before enjoying.

Banana Muffins With Chocolate Chips

Servings: 8
Cooking Time: 25 Minutes
Ingredients:

- 1 cup flour
- ½ tsp baking soda
- 1/3 cup brown sugar
- ¼ tsp salt
- 1/3 cup mashed banana
- ½ tsp vanilla extract
- 1 egg
- 1 tbsp vegetable oil
- ¼ cup chocolate chips
- 1 tbsp powdered sugar

Directions:

1. Preheat air fryer at 375ºF. Combine dry ingredients in a bowl. In another bowl, mix wet ingredients. Pour wet ingredients into dry ingredients and gently toss to combine. Fold in chocolate chips. Do not overmix.

2. Spoon mixture into 8 greased silicone cupcake liners, place them in the frying basket, and Bake for 6-8 minutes. Let cool onto a cooling rack. Serve right away sprinkled with powdered sugar.

Roasted Vegetable Frittata

Servings: 1
Cooking Time: 19 Minutes
Ingredients:

- ½ red or green bell pepper, cut into ½-inch chunks
- 4 button mushrooms, sliced
- ½ cup diced zucchini
- ½ teaspoon chopped fresh oregano or thyme
- 1 teaspoon olive oil
- 3 eggs, beaten
- ½ cup grated Cheddar cheese
- salt and freshly ground black pepper, to taste
- 1 teaspoon butter
- 1 teaspoon chopped fresh parsley

Directions:

1. Preheat the air fryer to 400°F.

2. Toss the peppers, mushrooms, zucchini and oregano with the olive oil and air-fry for 6 minutes, shaking the basket once or twice during the cooking process to redistribute the ingredients.

3. While the vegetables are cooking, beat the eggs well in a bowl, stir in the Cheddar cheese and season with salt and freshly ground black pepper. Add the air-fried vegetables to this bowl when they have finished cooking.

4. Place a 6- or 7-inch non-stick metal cake pan into the air fryer basket with the butter using an aluminum sling to lower the pan into the basket. (Fold a piece of aluminum foil into a strip about 2-inches wide by 24-inches long.) Air-fry for 1 minute at 380°F to melt the butter. Remove the cake pan and rotate the pan to distribute the butter and grease the pan. Pour the egg mixture into the cake pan and return the pan to the air fryer, using the aluminum sling.

5. Air-fry at 380°F for 12 minutes, or until the frittata has puffed up and is lightly browned. Let the frittata sit in the air fryer for 5 minutes to cool to an edible temperature and set up. Remove the cake pan from the air fryer, sprinkle with parsley and serve immediately.

Oat Bran Muffins

Servings: 8

Cooking Time: 12 Minutes

Ingredients:

- ⅔ cup oat bran
- ½ cup flour
- ¼ cup brown sugar
- 1 teaspoon baking powder
- ½ teaspoon baking soda
- ⅛ teaspoon salt
- ½ cup buttermilk
- 1 egg
- 2 tablespoons canola oil
- ½ cup chopped dates, raisins, or dried cranberries
- 24 paper muffin cups
- cooking spray

Directions:

1. Preheat air fryer to 330°F.
2. In a large bowl, combine the oat bran, flour, brown sugar, baking powder, baking soda, and salt.
3. In a small bowl, beat together the buttermilk, egg, and oil.
4. Pour buttermilk mixture into bowl with dry ingredients and stir just until moistened. Do not beat.
5. Gently stir in dried fruit.
6. Use triple baking cups to help muffins hold shape during baking. Spray them with cooking spray, place 4 sets of cups in air fryer basket at a time, and fill each one ¾ full of batter.
7. Cook for 12minutes, until top springs back when lightly touched and toothpick inserted in center comes out clean.
8. Repeat for remaining muffins.

Mashed Potato Taquitos With Hot Sauce

Servings: 4

Cooking Time: 30 Minutes

Ingredients:

- 1 potato, peeled and cubed
- 2 tbsp milk
- 2 garlic cloves, minced
- Salt and pepper to taste
- ½ tsp ground cumin
- 2 tbsp minced scallions
- 4 corn tortillas
- 1 cup red chili sauce
- 1 avocado, sliced
- 2 tbsp cilantro, chopped

Directions:

1. In a pot fitted with a steamer basket, cook the potato cubes for 15 minutes on the stovetop. Pour the potato cubes into a bowl and mash with a potato masher. Add the milk, garlic, salt, pepper, and cumin and stir. Add the scallions and cilantro and stir them into the mixture.
2. Preheat air fryer to 390°F. Run the tortillas under water for a second, then place them in the greased frying basket. Air Fry for 1 minute. Lay the tortillas on a flat surface. Place an equal amount of the potato filling in the center of each. Roll the tortilla sides over the filling and place seam-side down in the frying basket. Fry for 7 minutes or until the tortillas are golden and slightly crisp. Serve with chili sauce and avocado slices. Enjoy!

Blueberry Pannenkoek (dutch Pancake)

Servings: 4

Cooking Time: 30 Minutes

Ingredients:

- 3 eggs, beaten
- ½ cup buckwheat flour
- ½ cup milk
- ½ tsp vanilla
- 1 ½ cups blueberries, crushed
- 2 tbsp powdered sugar

Directions:

1.   Preheat air fryer to 330°F. Mix together eggs, buckwheat flour, milk, and vanilla in a bowl. Pour the batter into a greased baking pan and add it to the fryer. Bake until the pancake is puffed and golden, 12-16 minutes. Remove the pan and flip the pancake over onto a plate. Add blueberries and powdered sugar as a topping and serve.

Farmers Market Quiche

Servings: 4

Cooking Time: 35 Minutes

Ingredients:

- 4 button mushrooms
- ¼ medium red bell pepper
- 1 teaspoon extra-virgin olive oil
- One 9-inch pie crust, at room temperature
- ¼ cup grated carrot
- ¼ cup chopped, fresh baby spinach leaves
- 3 eggs, whisked
- ¼ cup half-and-half
- ½ teaspoon thyme
- ½ teaspoon sea salt
- 2 ounces crumbled goat cheese or feta

Directions:

1.   In a medium bowl, toss the mushrooms and bell pepper with extra-virgin olive oil; place into the air fryer basket. Set the temperature to 400°F for 8 minutes, stirring after 4 minutes. Remove from the air fryer, and roughly chop the mushrooms and bell peppers. Wipe the air fryer clean.

2.   Prep a 7-inch oven-safe baking dish by spraying the bottom of the pan with cooking spray.

3.   Place the pie crust into the baking dish; fold over and crimp the edges or use a fork to press to give the edges some shape.

4.   In a medium bowl, mix together the mushrooms, bell peppers, carrots, spinach, and eggs. Stir in the half-and-half, thyme, and salt.

5.   Pour the quiche mixture into the base of the pie shell. Top with crumbled cheese.

6.   Place the quiche into the air fryer basket. Set the temperature to 325°F for 30 minutes.

7.   When complete, turn the quiche halfway and cook an additional 5 minutes. Allow the quiche to rest 20 minutes prior to slicing and serving.

Ham And Cheddar Gritters

Servings: 6
Cooking Time: 12 Minutes
Ingredients:

- 4 cups water
- 1 cup quick-cooking grits
- ¼ teaspoon salt
- 2 tablespoons butter
- 2 cups grated Cheddar cheese, divided
- 1 cup finely diced ham
- 1 tablespoon chopped chives
- salt and freshly ground black pepper
- 1 egg, beaten
- 2 cups panko breadcrumbs
- vegetable oil

Directions:

1. Bring the water to a boil in a saucepan. Whisk in the grits and ¼ teaspoon of salt, and cook for 7 minutes until the grits are soft. Remove the pan from the heat and stir in the butter and 1 cup of the grated Cheddar cheese. Transfer the grits to a bowl and let them cool for just 10 to 15 minutes.
2. Stir the ham, chives and the rest of the cheese into the grits and season with salt and pepper to taste. Add the beaten egg and refrigerate the mixture for 30 minutes. (Try not to chill the grits much longer than 30 minutes, or the mixture will be too firm to shape into patties.)
3. While the grit mixture is chilling, make the country gravy and set it aside.
4. Place the panko breadcrumbs in a shallow dish. Measure out ¼-cup portions of the grits mixture and shape them into patties. Coat all sides of the patties with the panko breadcrumbs, patting them with your hands so the crumbs adhere to the patties. You should have about 16 patties. Spray both sides of the patties with oil.
5. Preheat the air fryer to 400°F.
6. In batches of 5 or 6, air-fry the fritters for 8 minutes. Using a flat spatula, flip the fritters over and air-fry for another 4 minutes.
7. Serve hot with country gravy.

Morning Chicken Frittata Cups

Servings:6
Cooking Time: 30 Minutes
Ingredients:

- ¼ cup shredded cooked chicken breasts
- 3 eggs
- 2 tbsp heavy cream
- 4 tsp Tabasco sauce
- ¼ cup grated Asiago cheese
- 2 tbsp chives, chopped

Directions:

1. Preheat air fryer to 350ºF. Beat all ingredients in a bowl. Divide the egg mixture between greased 6 muffin cups and place them in the frying basket. Bake for 8-10 minutes until set. Let cool slightly before serving. Enjoy!

Spinach And Artichoke White Pizza

Servings: 2
Cooking Time: 18 Minutes

Ingredients:

- olive oil
- 3 cups fresh spinach
- 2 cloves garlic, minced, divided
- 1 (6- to 8-ounce) pizza dough ball*
- ½ cup grated mozzarella cheese
- ¼ cup grated Fontina cheese
- ¼ cup artichoke hearts, coarsely chopped
- 2 tablespoons grated Parmesan cheese
- ¼ teaspoon dried oregano
- salt and freshly ground black pepper

Directions:

1. Heat the oil in a medium sauté pan on the stovetop. Add the spinach and half the minced garlic to the pan and sauté for a few minutes, until the spinach has wilted. Remove the sautéed spinach from the pan and set it aside.
2. Preheat the air fryer to 390°F.
3. Cut out a piece of aluminum foil the same size as the bottom of the air fryer basket. Brush the foil circle with olive oil. Shape the dough into a circle and place it on top of the foil. Dock the dough by piercing it several times with a fork. Brush the dough lightly with olive oil and transfer it into the air fryer basket with the foil on the bottom.
4. Air-fry the plain pizza dough for 6 minutes. Turn the dough over, remove the aluminum foil and brush again with olive oil. Air-fry for an additional 4 minutes.
5. Sprinkle the mozzarella and Fontina cheeses over the dough. Top with the spinach and artichoke hearts. Sprinkle the Parmesan cheese and dried oregano on top and drizzle with olive oil. Lower the temperature of the air fryer to 350°F and cook for 8 minutes, until the cheese has melted and is lightly browned. Season to taste with salt and freshly ground black pepper.

Mediterranean Egg Sandwich

Servings: 1
Cooking Time: 8 Minutes

Ingredients:

- 1 large egg
- 5 baby spinach leaves, chopped
- 1 tablespoon roasted bell pepper, chopped
- 1 English muffin
- 1 thin slice prosciutto or Canadian bacon

Directions:

1. Spray a ramekin with cooking spray or brush the inside with extra-virgin olive oil.
2. In a small bowl, whisk together the egg, baby spinach, and bell pepper.
3. Split the English muffin in half and spray the inside lightly with cooking spray or brush with extra-virgin olive oil.
4. Preheat the air fryer to 350°F for 2 minutes. Place the egg ramekin and open English muffin into the air fryer basket, and cook at 350°F for 5 minutes. Open the air fryer drawer and add the prosciutto or bacon; cook for an additional 1 minute.
5. To assemble the sandwich, place the egg on one half of the English muffin, top with prosciutto or bacon, and place the remaining piece of English muffin on top.

Peach Fritters

Servings: 8

Cooking Time: 6 Minutes

Ingredients:

- 1½ cups bread flour
- 1 teaspoon active dry yeast
- ¼ cup sugar
- ¼ teaspoon salt
- ½ cup warm milk
- ½ teaspoon vanilla extract
- 2 egg yolks
- 2 tablespoons melted butter
- 2 cups small diced peaches (fresh or frozen)
- 1 tablespoon butter
- 1 teaspoon ground cinnamon
- 1 to 2 tablespoons sugar
- Glaze
- ¾ cup powdered sugar
- 4 teaspoons milk

Directions:

1. Combine the flour, yeast, sugar and salt in a bowl. Add the milk, vanilla, egg yolks and melted butter and combine until the dough starts to come together. Transfer the dough to a floured surface and knead it by hand for 2 minutes. Shape the dough into a ball, place it in a large oiled bowl, cover with a clean kitchen towel and let the dough rise in a warm place for 1 to 1½ hours, or until the dough has doubled in size.

2. While the dough is rising, melt one tablespoon of butter in a medium saucepan on the stovetop. Add the diced peaches, cinnamon and sugar to taste. Cook the peaches for about 5 minutes, or until they soften. Set the peaches aside to cool.

3. When the dough has risen, transfer it to a floured surface and shape it into a 12-inch circle. Spread the peaches over half of the circle and fold the other half of the dough over the top. With a knife or a board scraper, score the dough by making slits in the dough in a diamond shape. Push the knife straight down into the dough and peaches, rather than slicing through. You should cut through the top layer of dough, but not the bottom. Roll the dough up into a log from one short end to the other. It should be roughly 8 inches long. Some of the peaches will be sticking out of the dough – don't worry, these are supposed to be a little random. Cut the log into 8 equal slices. Place the dough disks on a floured cookie sheet, cover with a clean kitchen towel and let rise in a warm place for 30 minutes.

4. Preheat the air fryer to 370°F.

5. Air-fry 2 or 3 fritters at a time at 370°F, for 3 minutes. Flip them over and continue to air-fry for another 2 to 3 minutes, until they are golden brown.

6. Combine the powdered sugar and milk together in a small bowl. Whisk vigorously until smooth. Allow the fritters to cool for at least 10 minutes and then brush the glaze over both the bottom and top of each one. Serve warm or at room temperature.

Appetizers And Snacks

Buffalo Chicken Wings

Servings: 6

Cooking Time: 60 Minutes

Ingredients:

- 2 lb chicken wings, split at the joint
- 1 tbsp butter, softened
- ½ cup buffalo wing sauce
- 1 tbs salt
- 1 tsp black pepper
- 1 tsp red chili powder
- 1 tsp garlic-ginger puree

Directions:

1. Preheat air fryer at 400ºF. Sprinkle the chicken wings with salt, pepper, red chili powder, grated garlic, and ginger. Place the chicken wings in the greased frying basket and Air Fry for 12 minutes, tossing once. Whisk butter and buffalo sauce in a large bowl. Air Fry for 10 more minutes, shaking once. Once done, transfer it into the bowl with the sauce. Serve immediately.

Spiced Parsnip Chips

Servings:2

Cooking Time: 35 Minutes

Ingredients:

- ½ tsp smoked paprika
- ¼ tsp chili powder
- ¼ tsp garlic powder
- ⅛ tsp onion powder
- ⅛ tsp cayenne pepper
- ⅛ tsp granulated sugar
- 1 tsp salt
- 1 parsnip, cut into chips
- 2 tsp olive oil

Directions:

1. Preheat air fryer to 400ºF. Mix all spices in a bowl and reserve. In another bowl, combine parsnip chips, olive oil, and salt. Place parsnip chips in the lightly greased frying basket and Air Fry for 12 minutes, shaking once. Transfer the chips to a bowl, toss in seasoning mix, and let sit for 15 minutes before serving.

Mouth-watering Vegetable Casserole

Servings: 3

Cooking Time: 45 Minutes

Ingredients:

- 1 red bell pepper, chopped
- ½ lb okra, trimmed
- 1 red onion, chopped
- 1 can diced tomatoes
- 2 tbsp balsamic vinegar
- 1 tbsp allspice
- 1 tsp ground cumin
- 1 cup baby spinach

Directions:

1. Preheat air fryer to 400°F. Combine the bell pepper, red onion, okra, tomatoes and juices, balsamic vinegar, allspice, and cumin in a baking pan and Roast for 25 minutes, stirring every 10 minutes. Stir in spinach and Roast for another 5 minutes. Serve warm.

Beer-battered Onion Rings

Servings: 4

Cooking Time: 25 Minutes

Ingredients:

- 2 sliced onions, rings separated
- 1 cup flour
- Salt and pepper to taste
- 1 tsp garlic powder
- 1 cup beer

Directions:

1. Preheat air fryer to 350°F. In a mixing bowl, combine the flour, garlic powder, beer, salt, and black pepper. Dip the onion rings into the bowl and lay the coated rings in the frying basket. Air Fry for 15 minutes, shaking the basket several times during cooking to jostle the onion rings and ensure a good even fry. Once ready, the onions should be crispy and golden brown. Serve hot.

Eggplant Fries

Servings: 4

Cooking Time: 8 Minutes

Ingredients:

- 1 medium eggplant
- 1 teaspoon ground coriander
- 1 teaspoon cumin
- 1 teaspoon garlic powder
- ½ teaspoon salt
- 1 cup crushed panko breadcrumbs
- 1 large egg
- 2 tablespoons water
- oil for misting or cooking spray

Directions:

1. Peel and cut the eggplant into fat fries, ⅜- to ½-inch thick.
2. Preheat air fryer to 390°F.
3. In a small cup, mix together the coriander, cumin, garlic, and salt.
4. Combine 1 teaspoon of the seasoning mix and panko crumbs in a shallow dish.
5. Place eggplant fries in a large bowl, sprinkle with remaining seasoning, and stir well to combine.
6. Beat eggs and water together and pour over eggplant fries. Stir to coat.
7. Remove eggplant from egg wash, shaking off excess, and roll in panko crumbs.
8. Spray with oil.
9. Place half of the fries in air fryer basket. You should have only a single layer, but it's fine if they overlap a little.
10. Cook for 5minutes. Shake basket, mist lightly with oil, and cook 3 minutes longer, until browned and crispy.
11. Repeat step 10 to cook remaining eggplant.

Fried Pickles

Servings: 2
Cooking Time: 15 Minutes
Ingredients:

- 1 egg
- 1 tablespoon milk
- ¼ teaspoon hot sauce
- 2 cups sliced dill pickles, well drained
- ¾ cup breadcrumbs
- oil for misting or cooking spray

Directions:

1. Preheat air fryer to 390°F.
2. Beat together egg, milk, and hot sauce in a bowl large enough to hold all the pickles.
3. Add pickles to the egg wash and stir well to coat.
4. Place breadcrumbs in a large plastic bag or container with lid.
5. Drain egg wash from pickles and place them in bag with breadcrumbs. Shake to coat.
6. Pile pickles into air fryer basket and spray with oil.
7. Cook for 5minutes. Shake basket and spray with oil.
8. Cook 5 more minutes. Shake and spray again. Separate any pickles that have stuck together and mist any spots you've missed.
9. Cook for 5minutes longer or until dark golden brown and crispy.

Warm And Salty Edamame

Servings: 4
Cooking Time: 10 Minutes
Ingredients:

- 1 pound Unshelled edamame
- Vegetable oil spray
- ¾ teaspoon Coarse sea salt or kosher salt

Directions:

1. Preheat the air fryer to 400°F.
2. Place the edamame in a large bowl and lightly coat them with vegetable oil spray. Toss well, spray again, and toss until they are evenly coated.
3. When the machine is at temperature, pour the edamame into the basket and air-fry, tossing the basket quite often to rearrange the edamame, for 7 minutes, or until warm and aromatic. (Air-fry for 10 minutes if the edamame were frozen and not thawed.)
4. Pour the edamame into a bowl and sprinkle the salt on top. Toss well, then set aside for a couple of minutes before serving with an empty bowl on the side for the pods.

Arancini With Sun-dried Tomatoes And Mozzarella

Servings: 6

Cooking Time: 15 Minutes

Ingredients:

- 1 tablespoon olive oil
- ½ small onion, finely chopped
- 1 cup Arborio rice
- ¼ cup white wine or dry vermouth
- 1 cup vegetable or chicken stock
- 1½ cups water
- 1 teaspoon salt
- freshly ground black pepper
- ⅓ cup grated Parmigiano-Reggiano cheese
- 2 to 3 ounces mozzarella cheese
- 2 eggs, lightly beaten
- ¼ cup chopped oil-packed sun-dried tomatoes
- 1½ cups Italian seasoned breadcrumbs, divided
- olive oil
- marinara sauce, for serving

Directions:

1. .Start by cooking the Arborio rice.

2. Stovetop Method: Preheat a medium saucepan over medium heat. Add the olive oil and sauté the onion until it starts to become tender – about 5 minutes. Add the rice and stir well to coat all the grains of rice. Add the white wine or vermouth. Let this simmer and get absorbed by the rice. Then add the stock and water, cover, reduce the heat to low and simmer for 20 minutes.

3. Pressure-Cooker Method: Preheat the pressure cooker using the BROWN setting. Add the oil and cook the onion for a few minutes. Add the rice, wine, stock, water, salt and freshly ground black pepper, give everything one good stir and lock the lid in place. Pressure cook on HIGH for 7 minutes. Reduce the pressure with the QUICK-RELEASE method and carefully remove the lid.

4. Taste the rice to make sure it is tender. Season with salt and freshly ground black pepper and stir in the grated Parmigiano-Reggiano cheese. Spread the rice out onto a baking sheet to cool.

5. While the rice is cooling, cut the mozzarella into ¾-inch cubes.

6. Once the rice has cooled, combine the rice with the eggs, sun-dried tomatoes and ½ cup of the breadcrumbs. Place the remaining breadcrumbs in a shallow dish. Shape the rice mixture into 12 balls. Press a hole in the rice ball with your finger and push one or two cubes of mozzarella cheese into the hole. Mold the rice back into a ball, enclosing the cheese. Roll the finished rice balls in the breadcrumbs and place them on a baking sheet while you make the remaining rice balls. Spray or brush the rice balls with olive oil.

7. Preheat the air fryer to 380°F.

8. Cook 6 arancini at a time. Air-fry for 10 minutes. Gently turn the arancini over, brush or spray with oil again and air-fry for another 5 minutes. Serve warm with the marinara sauce.

Easy Crab Cakes

Servings: 4
Cooking Time: 20 Minutes
Ingredients:

- 1 cup lump crab meat
- 2 green onions, minced
- 3 garlic cloves, minced
- ½ lime, juiced
- 2 tbsp mayonnaise
- 2 eggs, beaten
- 1 tsp fresh grated ginger
- ½ tsp allspice
- ½ cup breadcrumbs
- 2 tsp oyster sauce
- 2 tsp spicy mustard
- Pinch of black pepper

Directions:

1. Preheat air fryer to 350°F. Place the crab meat, lime juice, mayonnaise, onions, garlic, ginger, oyster sauce, mustard, allspice, and black pepper in a large mixing bowl. Stir thoroughly until all the ingredients are evenly combined.

2. Form the mixture into patties. Dip the patties into the beaten eggs, and then roll in the breadcrumbs, coating thoroughly on all sides. Place the coated cakes in the lined frying basket and Air Fry for 5 minutes. Flip the cakes over and cook for another 5 minutes until golden brown and crispy on the outside and tantalizingly juicy on the inside. Serve hot.

Savory Sausage Balls

Servings: 10
Cooking Time: 8 Minutes
Ingredients:

- 2 cups all-purpose flour
- 1 tablespoon baking powder
- ½ teaspoon garlic powder
- ¼ teaspoon onion powder
- ½ teaspoon salt
- 3 tablespoons milk
- 2½ cups grated pepper jack cheese
- 1 pound fresh sausage, casing removed

Directions:

1. Preheat the air fryer to 370°F.

2. In a large bowl, whisk together the flour, baking powder, garlic powder, onion powder, and salt. Add in the milk, grated cheese, and sausage.

3. Using a tablespoon, scoop out the sausage and roll it between your hands to form a rounded ball. You should end up with approximately 32 balls. Place them in the air fryer basket in a single layer and working in batches as necessary.

4. Cook for 8 minutes, or until the outer coating turns light brown.

5. Carefully remove, repeating with the remaining sausage balls.

Honey-mustard Chicken Wings

Servings: 2

Cooking Time: 14 Minutes

Ingredients:

- 2 pounds chicken wings
- salt and freshly ground black pepper
- 2 tablespoons butter
- ¼ cup honey
- ¼ cup spicy brown mustard
- pinch ground cayenne pepper
- 2 teaspoons Worcestershire sauce

Directions:

1. Prepare the chicken wings by cutting off the wing tips and discarding (or freezing for chicken stock). Divide the drumettes from the wingettes by cutting through the joint. Place the chicken wing pieces in a large bowl.

2. Preheat the air fryer to 400°F.

3. Season the wings with salt and freshly ground black pepper and air-fry the wings in two batches for 10 minutes per batch, shaking the basket half way through the cooking process.

4. While the wings are air-frying, combine the remaining ingredients in a small saucepan over low heat.

5. When both batches are done, toss all the wings with the honey-mustard sauce and toss them all back into the basket for another 4 minutes to heat through and finish cooking. Give the basket a good shake part way through the cooking process to redistribute the wings. Remove the wings from the air fryer and serve.

Italian Bruschetta With Mushrooms & Cheese

Servings: 4

Cooking Time: 25 Minutes

Ingredients:

- ½ cup button mushrooms, chopped
- ½ baguette, sliced
- 1 garlic clove, minced
- 3 oz sliced Parmesan cheese
- 1 tbsp extra virgin olive oil
- Salt and pepper to taste

Directions:

1. Preheat air fryer to 350°F. Add the mushrooms, olive oil, salt, pepper, and garlic to a mixing bowl and stir thoroughly to combine. Divide the mushroom mixture between the bread slices, drizzling all over the surface with olive oil, then cover with Parmesan slices. Place the covered bread slices in the greased frying basket and Bake for 15 minutes. Serve and enjoy!

Crispy Wontons

Servings: 8

Cooking Time: 10 Minutes

Ingredients:

- ½ cup refried beans
- 3 tablespoons salsa
- ¼ cup canned artichoke hearts, drained and patted dry
- ¼ cup frozen spinach, defrosted and squeezed dry
- 2 ounces cream cheese
- 1½ teaspoons dried oregano, divided
- ¼ teaspoon garlic powder
- ¼ teaspoon onion powder
- ½ teaspoon salt
- ¼ cup chopped pepperoni
- ¼ cup grated mozzarella cheese
- 1 tablespoon grated Parmesan
- 2 ounces cream cheese
- ½ teaspoon dried oregano
- 32 wontons
- 1 cup water

Directions:

1. Preheat the air fryer to 370°F.

2. In a medium bowl, mix together the refried beans and salsa.

3. In a second medium bowl, mix together the artichoke hearts, spinach, cream cheese, oregano, garlic powder, onion powder, and salt.

4. In a third medium bowl, mix together the pepperoni, mozzarella cheese, Parmesan cheese, cream cheese, and the remaining ½ teaspoon of oregano.

5. Get a towel lightly damp with water and ring it out. While working with the wontons, leave the unfilled wontons under the damp towel so they don't dry out.

6. Working with 8 wontons at a time, place 2 teaspoons of one of the fillings into the center of the wonton, rotating among the different fillings (one filling per wonton). Working one at a time, use a pastry brush, dip the pastry brush into the water, and brush the edges of the dough with the water. Fold the dough in half to form a triangle and set aside. Continue until 8 wontons are formed. Spray the wontons with cooking spray and cover with a dry towel. Repeat until all 32 wontons have been filled.

7. Place the wontons into the air fryer basket, leaving space between the wontons, and cook for 5 minutes. Turn over and check for brownness, and then cook for another 5 minutes.

Baba Ghanouj

Servings: 2

Cooking Time: 40 Minutes

Ingredients:

- 2 Small (12-ounce) purple Italian eggplant(s)
- ¼ cup Olive oil
- ¼ cup Tahini
- ½ teaspoon Ground black pepper
- ¼ teaspoon Onion powder
- ¼ teaspoon Mild smoked paprika (optional)
- Up to 1 teaspoon Table salt

Directions:

1. Preheat the air fryer to 400°F.

2. Prick the eggplant(s) on all sides with a fork. When the machine is at temperature, set the eggplant(s) in the basket in one layer. Air-fry undisturbed for 40 minutes, or until blackened and soft.

3. Remove the basket from the machine. Cool the eggplant(s) in the basket for 20 minutes.

4. Use a nonstick-safe spatula, and perhaps a flatware tablespoon for balance, to gently transfer the eggplant(s) to a bowl. The juices will run out. Make sure the bowl is close to the basket. Split the eggplant(s) open.

5. Scrape the soft insides of half an eggplant into a food processor. Repeat with the remaining piece(s). Add any juices from the bowl to the eggplant in the food processor, but discard the skins and stems.

6. Add the olive oil, tahini, pepper, onion powder, and smoked paprika (if using). Add about half the salt, then cover and process until smooth, stopping the machine at least once to scrape down the inside of the canister. Check the spread for salt and add more as needed. Scrape the baba ghanouj into a bowl and serve warm, or set aside at room temperature for up to 2 hours, or cover and store in the refrigerator for up to 4 days.

Home-style Taro Chips

Servings: 2

Cooking Time: 20 Minutes

Ingredients:

- 1 tbsp olive oil
- 1 cup thinly sliced taro
- Salt to taste
- ½ cup hummus

Directions:

1. Preheat air fryer to 325°F. Put the sliced taro in the greased frying basket, spread the pieces out, and drizzle with olive oil. Air Fry for 10-12 minutes, shaking the basket twice. Sprinkle with salt and serve with hummus.

Mini Frank Rolls

Servings: 4

Cooking Time: 30 Minutes

Ingredients:

- ½ can crescent rolls
- 8 mini smoked hot dogs
- ½ tsp dried rosemary

Directions:

1. Preheat air fryer to 350°F. Roll out the crescent roll dough and separate into 8 triangles. Cut each triangle in half. Place 1 hot dog at the base of the triangle and roll it up in the dough; gently press the tip in. Repeat for the rest of the rolls. Place the rolls in the greased frying basket and sprinkle with rosemary. Bake for 8-10 minutes. Serve warm. Enjoy!

Poppy Seed Mini Hot Dog Rolls

Servings: 4

Cooking Time: 25 Minutes

Ingredients:

- 8 small mini hot dogs
- 8 pastry dough sheets
- 1 tbsp vegetable oil
- 1 tbsp poppy seeds

Directions:

1. Preheat the air fryer to 350°F. Roll the mini hot dogs into a pastry dough sheet, wrapping them snugly. Brush the rolls with vegetable oil on all sides. Arrange them on the frying basket and sprinkle poppy seeds on top. Bake for 15 minutes until the pastry crust is golden brown. Serve.

Mozzarella En Carrozza With Puttanesca Sauce

Servings: 6

Cooking Time: 8 Minutes

Ingredients:

- Puttanesca Sauce
- 2 teaspoons olive oil
- 1 anchovy, chopped (optional)
- 2 cloves garlic, minced
- 1 (14-ounce) can petite diced tomatoes
- ½ cup chicken stock or water
- ⅓ cup Kalamata olives, chopped
- 2 tablespoons capers
- ½ teaspoon dried oregano
- ¼ teaspoon crushed red pepper flakes
- salt and freshly ground black pepper
- 1 tablespoon fresh parsley, chopped
- 8 slices of thinly sliced white bread (Pepperidge Farm®)
- 8 ounces mozzarella cheese, cut into ¼-inch slices
- ½ cup all-purpose flour
- 3 eggs, beaten
- 1½ cups seasoned panko breadcrumbs
- ½ teaspoon garlic powder
- ½ teaspoon salt
- freshly ground black pepper
- olive oil, in a spray bottle

Directions:

1. Start by making the puttanesca sauce. Heat the olive oil in a medium saucepan on the stovetop. Add the anchovies (if using, and I really think you should!) and garlic and sauté for 3 minutes, or until the anchovies have "melted" into the oil. Add the tomatoes, chicken stock, olives, capers, oregano and crushed red pepper flakes and simmer the sauce for 20 minutes. Season with salt and freshly ground black pepper and stir in the fresh parsley.

2. Cut the crusts off the slices of bread. Place four slices of the bread on a cutting board. Divide the cheese between the four slices of bread. Top the cheese with the remaining four slices of bread to make little sandwiches and cut each sandwich into 4 triangles.

3. Set up a dredging station using three shallow dishes. Place the flour in the first shallow dish, the eggs in the second dish and in the third dish, combine the panko breadcrumbs, garlic powder, salt and black pepper. Dredge each little triangle in the flour first (you might think this is redundant, but it helps to get the coating to adhere to the edges of the sandwiches) and then dip them into the egg, making sure both the sides and the edges are coated. Let the excess egg drip off and then press the triangles into the breadcrumb mixture, pressing the crumbs on with your hands so they adhere. Place the coated triangles in the freezer for 2 hours, until the cheese is frozen.

4. Preheat the air fryer to 390°F. Spray all sides of the mozzarella triangles with oil and transfer a single layer of triangles to the air fryer basket. Air-fry in batches at 390°F for 5 minutes. Turn the triangles over and air-fry for an additional 3 minutes.

5. Serve mozzarella triangles immediately with the warm puttanesca sauce.

Sugar-glazed Walnuts

Servings: 6

Cooking Time: 5 Minutes

Ingredients:

- 1 Large egg white(s)
- 2 tablespoons Granulated white sugar
- ⅛ teaspoon Table salt
- 2 cups (7 ounces) Walnut halves

Directions:

1. Preheat the air fryer to 400°F.
2. Use a whisk to beat the egg white(s) in a large bowl until quite foamy, more so than just well combined but certainly not yet a meringue.
3. If you're working with the quantities for a small batch, remove half of the foamy egg white.
4. If you're working with the quantities for a large batch, remove a quarter of it. It's fine to eyeball the amounts.
5. You can store the removed egg white in a sealed container to save for another use.
6. Stir in the sugar and salt. Add the walnut halves and toss to coat evenly and well, including the nuts' crevasses.
7. When the machine is at temperature, use a slotted spoon to transfer the walnut halves to the basket, taking care not to dislodge any coating. Gently spread the nuts into as close to one layer as you can. Air-fry undisturbed for 2 minutes.
8. Break up any clumps, toss the walnuts gently but well, and air-fry for 3 minutes more, tossing after 1 minute, then every 30 seconds thereafter, until the nuts are browned in spots and very aromatic. Watch carefully so they don't burn.
9. Gently dump the nuts onto a lipped baking sheet and spread them into one layer. Cool for at least 10 minutes before serving, separating any that stick together. The walnuts can be stored in a sealed container at room temperature for up to 5 days.

Smoked Salmon Puffs

Servings: 2

Cooking Time: 8 Minutes

Ingredients:

- Two quarters of one thawed sheet (that is, a half of the sheet; wrap and refreeze the remainder) A 17.25-ounce box frozen puff pastry
- 4 ½-ounce smoked salmon slices
- 2 tablespoons Softened regular or low-fat cream cheese (not fat-free)
- Up to 2 teaspoons Drained and rinsed capers, minced
- Up to 2 teaspoons Minced red onion
- 1 Large egg white
- 1 tablespoon Water

Directions:

1. Preheat the air fryer to 400°F.
2. For a small air fryer, roll the piece of puff pastry into a 6 x 6-inch square on a clean, dry work surface.
3. For a medium or larger air fryer, roll each piece of puff pastry into a 6 x 6-inch square.
4. Set 2 salmon slices on the diagonal, corner to corner, on each rolled-out sheet. Smear the salmon with cream cheese, then sprinkle with capers and red onion. Fold the sheet closed by picking up one corner that does not have an edge of salmon near it and folding the dough across the salmon to its opposite corner. Seal the edges closed by pressing the tines of a flatware fork into them.
5. Whisk the egg white and water in a small bowl until uniform. Brush this mixture over the top(s) of the packet(s).
6. Set the packet(s) in the basket (if you're working with more than one, they cannot touch). Air-fry undisturbed for 8 minutes, or until golden brown and flaky.
7. Use a nonstick-safe spatula to transfer the packet(s) to a wire rack. Cool for 5 minutes before serving.

Poultry Recipes

Honey-glazed Cornish Hen

Servings:2
Cooking Time: 40 Minutes
Ingredients:

- 2 tbsp butter, melted
- 2 tbsp Dijon mustard
- Salt and pepper to taste
- ⅛ tsp ground nutmeg
- ½ tsp honey
- 1 tbsp olive oil
- 1 Cornish game hen
- 1 tangerine, quartered

Directions:

1. Preheat air fryer to 350ºF. Whisk the butter, mustard, salt, black pepper, nutmeg, and honey in a bowl. Brush olive oil over and inside of cornish hen and scatter with the honey mixture. Stuff tangerine into the hen´s cavity.

2. Place hen in the frying basket and Air Fry for 28-32 minutes, flipping twice. Transfer it to a cutting board and let rest for 5 minutes until easy to handle. Split in half by cutting down the spine and serve right away.

Asian Meatball Tacos

Servings: 4
Cooking Time: 10 Minutes
Ingredients:

- 1 pound lean ground turkey
- 3 tablespoons soy sauce
- 1 tablespoon brown sugar
- ½ teaspoon onion powder
- ½ teaspoon garlic powder
- 1 tablespoon sesame seeds
- 1 English cucumber
- 4 radishes
- 2 tablespoons white wine vinegar
- 1 lime, juiced and divided
- 1 tablespoon avocado oil
- Salt, to taste
- ½ cup Greek yogurt
- 1 to 3 teaspoons Sriracha, based on desired spiciness
- 1 cup shredded cabbage
- ¼ cup chopped cilantro
- Eight 6-inch flour tortillas

Directions:

1. Preheat the air fryer to 360°F.

2. In a large bowl, mix the ground turkey, soy sauce, brown sugar, onion powder, garlic powder, and sesame seeds. Form the meat into 1-inch meatballs and place in the air fryer basket. Cook for 5 minutes, shake the basket, and cook another 5 minutes. Using a food thermometer, make sure the internal temperature of the meatballs is 165°F.

3. Meanwhile, dice the cucumber and radishes and place in a medium bowl. Add the white wine vinegar, 1 teaspoon of the lime juice, and the avocado oil, and stir to coat. Season with salt to desired taste.

4. In a large bowl, mix the Greek yogurt, Sriracha, and the remaining lime juice, and stir. Add in the cabbage and cilantro; toss well to create a slaw.

5. In a heavy skillet, heat the tortillas over medium heat for 1 to 2 minutes on each side, or until warmed.

6. To serve, place a tortilla on a plate, top with 5 meatballs, then with cucumber and radish salad, and finish with 2 tablespoons of cabbage slaw.

Honey Lemon Thyme Glazed Cornish Hen

Servings: 2
Cooking Time: 20 Minutes
Ingredients:

- 1 (2-pound) Cornish game hen, split in half
- olive oil
- salt and freshly ground black pepper
- ¼ teaspoon dried thyme
- ¼ cup honey
- 1 tablespoon lemon zest
- juice of 1 lemon
- 1½ teaspoons chopped fresh thyme leaves
- ½ teaspoon soy sauce
- freshly ground black pepper

Directions:

1. Split the game hen in half by cutting down each side of the backbone and then cutting through the breast. Brush or spray both halves of the game hen with the olive oil and then season with the salt, pepper and dried thyme.
2. Preheat the air fryer to 390°F.
3. Place the game hen, skin side down, into the air fryer and air-fry for 5 minutes. Turn the hen halves over and air-fry for 10 minutes.
4. While the hen is cooking, combine the honey, lemon zest and juice, fresh thyme, soy sauce and pepper in a small bowl.
5. When the air fryer timer rings, brush the honey glaze onto the game hen and continue to air-fry for another 3 to 5 minutes, just until the hen is nicely glazed, browned and has an internal temperature of 165°F.
6. Let the hen rest for 5 minutes and serve warm.

Cajun Chicken Kebabs

Servings: 4
Cooking Time: 30 Minutes
Ingredients:

- 3 tbsp lemon juice
- 2 tsp olive oil
- 2 tbsp chopped parsley
- ½ tsp dried oregano
- ½ Cajun seasoning
- 1 lb chicken breasts, cubed
- 1 cup cherry tomatoes
- 1 zucchini, cubed

Directions:

1. Preheat air fryer to 400°F. Combine the lemon juice, olive oil, parsley, oregano, and Cajun seasoning in a bowl. Toss in the chicken and stir, making sure all pieces are coated. Allow to marinate for 10 minutes. Take 8 bamboo skewers and poke the chicken, tomatoes, and zucchini, alternating the pieces. Use a brush to put more marinade on them, then lay them in the air fryer. Air Fry the kebabs for 15 minutes, turning once, or until the chicken is cooked through, with no pink showing. Get rid of the leftover marinade. Serve and enjoy!

Parmesan Crusted Chicken Cordon Bleu

Servings: 2

Cooking Time: 14 Minutes

Ingredients:

- 2 (6-ounce) boneless, skinless chicken breasts
- salt and freshly ground black pepper
- 1 tablespoon Dijon mustard
- 4 slices Swiss cheese
- 4 slices deli-sliced ham
- ¼ cup all-purpose flour*
- 1 egg, beaten
- ¾ cup panko breadcrumbs*
- ⅓ cup grated Parmesan cheese
- olive oil, in a spray bottle

Directions:

1. Butterfly the chicken breasts. Place the chicken breast on a cutting board and press down on the breast with the palm of your hand. Slice into the long side of the chicken breast, parallel to the cutting board, but not all the way through to the other side. Open the chicken breast like a "book". Place a piece of plastic wrap over the chicken breast and gently pound it with a meat mallet to make it evenly thick.

2. Season the chicken with salt and pepper. Spread the Dijon mustard on the inside of each chicken breast. Layer one slice of cheese on top of the mustard, then top with the 2 slices of ham and the other slice of cheese.

3. Starting with the long edge of the chicken breast, roll the chicken up to the other side. Secure it shut with 1 or 2 toothpicks.

4. Preheat the air fryer to 350°F.

5. Set up a dredging station with three shallow dishes. Place the flour in the first dish. Place the beaten egg in the second shallow dish. Combine the panko breadcrumbs and Parmesan cheese together in the third shallow dish. Dip the stuffed and rolled chicken breasts in the flour, then the beaten egg and then roll in the breadcrumb-cheese mixture to cover on all sides. Press the crumbs onto the chicken breasts with your hands to make sure they are well adhered. Spray the chicken breasts with olive oil and transfer to the air fryer basket.

6. Air-fry at 350°F for 14 minutes, flipping the breasts over halfway through the cooking time. Let the chicken rest for a few minutes before removing the toothpicks, slicing and serving.

Nacho Chicken Fries

Servings: 4

Cooking Time: 7 Minutes

Ingredients:

- 1 pound chicken tenders
- salt
- ¼ cup flour
- 2 eggs
- ¾ cup panko breadcrumbs
- ¾ cup crushed organic nacho cheese tortilla chips
- oil for misting or cooking spray
- Seasoning Mix
- 1 tablespoon chili powder
- 1 teaspoon ground cumin
- ½ teaspoon garlic powder
- ½ teaspoon onion powder

Directions:

1. Stir together all seasonings in a small cup and set aside.
2. Cut chicken tenders in half crosswise, then cut into strips no wider than about ½ inch.
3. Preheat air fryer to 390°F.
4. Salt chicken to taste. Place strips in large bowl and sprinkle with 1 tablespoon of the seasoning mix. Stir well to distribute seasonings.
5. Add flour to chicken and stir well to coat all sides.
6. Beat eggs together in a shallow dish.
7. In a second shallow dish, combine the panko, crushed chips, and the remaining 2 teaspoons of seasoning mix.
8. Dip chicken strips in eggs, then roll in crumbs. Mist with oil or cooking spray.
9. Chicken strips will cook best if done in two batches. They can be crowded and overlapping a little but not stacked in double or triple layers.
10. Cook for 4minutes. Shake basket, mist with oil, and cook 3 moreminutes, until chicken juices run clear and outside is crispy.
11. Repeat step 10 to cook remaining chicken fries.

Indian Chicken Tandoori

Servings: 2

Cooking Time: 35 Minutes

Ingredients:

- 2 chicken breasts, cubed
- ½ cup hung curd
- 1 tsp turmeric powder
- 1 tsp red chili powder
- 1 tsp chaat masala powder
- Pinch of salt

Directions:

1. Preheat air fryer to 350°F. Mix the hung curd, turmeric, red chili powder, chaat masala powder, and salt in a mixing bowl. Stir until the mixture is free of lumps. Coat the chicken with the mixture, cover, and refrigerate for 30 minutes to marinate. Place the marinated chicken chunks in a baking pan and drizzle with the remaining marinade. Bake for 25 minutes until the chicken is juicy and spiced. Serve warm.

Japanese-inspired Glazed Chicken

Servings: 4
Cooking Time: 25 Minutes
Ingredients:

- 4 chicken breasts
- Chicken seasoning to taste
- Salt and pepper to taste
- 2 tsp grated fresh ginger
- 2 garlic cloves, minced
- ¼ cup molasses
- 2 tbsp tamari sauce

Directions:

1. Preheat air fryer to 400°F. Season the chicken with seasoning, salt, and pepper. Place the chicken in the greased frying basket and Air Fry for 7 minutes, then flip the chicken. Cook for another 3 minutes.

2. While the chicken is cooking, combine ginger, garlic, molasses, and tamari sauce in a saucepan over medium heat. Cook for 4 minutes or until the sauce thickens. Transfer all of the chicken to a serving dish. Drizzle with ginger-tamari glaze and serve.

Sage & Paprika Turkey Cutlets

Servings: 4
Cooking Time: 15 Minutes
Ingredients:

- ½ cup bread crumbs
- ¼ tsp paprika
- Salt and pepper to taste
- ⅛ tsp dried sage
- ⅛ tsp garlic powder
- ¼ tsp ground cumin
- 1 egg
- 4 turkey breast cutlets
- 2 tbsp chopped chervil

Directions:

1. Preheat air fryer to 380°F. Combine the bread crumbs, paprika, salt, black pepper, sage, cumin, and garlic powder in a bowl and mix well. Beat the egg in another bowl until frothy. Dip the turkey cutlets into the egg mixture, then coat them in the bread crumb mixture. Put the breaded turkey cutlets in the frying basket. Bake for 4 minutes. Turn the cutlets over, then Bake for 4 more minutes. Decorate with chervil and serve.

Chicken Fried Steak With Gravy

Servings: 4

Cooking Time: 10 Minutes Per Batch

Ingredients:

- ½ cup flour
- 2 teaspoons salt, divided
- freshly ground black pepper
- ¼ teaspoon garlic powder
- 1 cup buttermilk
- 1 cup fine breadcrumbs
- 4 tenderized top round steaks (about 6 to 8 ounces each; ½-inch thick)
- vegetable or canola oil
- For the Gravy:
- 2 tablespoons butter or bacon drippings
- ¼ onion, minced (about ¼ cup)
- 1 clove garlic, smashed
- ¼ teaspoon dried thyme
- 3 tablespoons flour
- 1 cup milk
- salt and lots of freshly ground black pepper
- a few dashes of Worcestershire sauce

Directions:

1. Set up a dredging station. Combine the flour, 1 teaspoon of salt, black pepper and garlic powder in a shallow bowl. Pour the buttermilk into a second shallow bowl. Finally, put the breadcrumbs and 1 teaspoon of salt in a third shallow bowl.

2. Dip the tenderized steaks into the flour, then the buttermilk, and then the breadcrumb mixture, pressing the crumbs onto the steak. Place them on a baking sheet and spray both sides generously with vegetable or canola oil.

3. Preheat the air fryer to 400°F.

4. Transfer the steaks to the air fryer basket, two at a time, and air-fry for 10 minutes, flipping the steaks over halfway through the cooking time. This will cook your steaks to medium. If you want the steaks cooked a little more or less, add or subtract a minute or two. Hold the first batch of steaks warm in a 170°F oven while you cook the second batch.

5. While the steaks are cooking, make the gravy. Melt the butter in a small saucepan over medium heat on the stovetop. Add the onion, garlic and thyme and cook for five minutes, until the onion is soft and just starting to brown. Stir in the flour and cook for another five minutes, stirring regularly, until the mixture starts to brown. Whisk in the milk and bring the mixture to a boil to thicken. Season to taste with salt, lots of freshly ground black pepper and a few dashes of Worcestershire sauce.

6. Plate the chicken fried steaks with mashed potatoes and vegetables and serve the gravy at the table to pour over the top.

Herb-marinated Chicken

Servings: 4

Cooking Time: 25 Minutes

Ingredients:

- 4 chicken breasts
- 2 tsp rosemary, minced
- 2 tsp thyme, minced
- Salt and pepper to taste
- ½ cup chopped cilantro
- 1 lime, juiced

Directions:

1. Place chicken in a resealable bag. Add rosemary, thyme, salt, pepper, cilantro, and lime juice. Seal the bag and toss to coat, then place in the refrigerator for 2 hours.

2. Preheat air fryer to 400°F. Arrange the chicken in a single layer in the greased frying basket. Spray the chicken with cooking oil. Air Fry for 6-7 minutes, then flip the chicken. Cook for another 3 minutes. Serve and enjoy!

Lemon Herb Whole Cornish Hen

Servings: 2

Cooking Time: 50 Minutes

Ingredients:

- 1 Cornish hen
- ¼ cup olive oil
- 2 tbsp lemon juice
- 2 tbsp sage, chopped
- 2 tbsp thyme, chopped
- 4 garlic cloves, chopped
- Salt and pepper to taste
- 1 celery stalk, chopped
- ½ small onion
- ½ lemon, juiced and zested
- 2 tbsp chopped parsley

Directions:

1. Preheat air fryer to 380°F. Whisk the olive oil, lemon juice, sage, thyme, garlic, salt, and pepper in a bowl. Rub the mixture on the tops and sides of the hen. Pour any excess inside the cavity of the bird. Stuff the celery, onion, and lemon juice and zest into the cavity of the hen. Put in the frying basket and Roast for 40-45 minutes. Cut the hen in half and serve garnished with parsley.

Chicken Tenders With Basil-strawberry Glaze

Servings:4

Cooking Time: 20 Minutes

Ingredients:

- 1 lb chicken tenderloins
- ¼ cup strawberry preserves
- 3 tbsp chopped basil
- 1 tsp orange juice
- ½ tsp orange zest
- Salt and pepper to taste

Directions:

1. Combine all ingredients, except for 1 tbsp of basil, in a bowl. Marinade in the fridge covered for 30 minutes.

2. Preheat air fryer to 350°F. Place the chicken tenders in the frying basket and Air Fry for 4-6 minutes. Shake gently the basket and turn over the chicken. Cook for 5 more minutes. Top with the remaining basil to serve.

Asian-style Orange Chicken

Servings: 4
Cooking Time: 25 Minutes
Ingredients:
- 1 lb chicken breasts, cubed
- Salt and pepper to taste
- 6 tbsp cornstarch
- 1 cup orange juice
- ¼ cup orange marmalade
- ¼ cup ketchup
- ½ tsp ground ginger
- 2 tbsp soy sauce
- 1 1/3 cups edamame beans

Directions:

1. Preheat the air fryer to 375°F. Sprinkle the cubes with salt and pepper. Coat with 4 tbsp of cornstarch and set aside on a wire rack. Mix the orange juice, marmalade, ketchup, ginger, soy sauce, and the remaining cornstarch in a cake pan, then stir in the beans. Set the pan in the frying basket and Bake for 5-8 minutes, stirring once during cooking until the sauce is thick and bubbling. Remove from the fryer and set aside. Put the chicken in the frying basket and fry for 10-12 minutes, shaking the basket once. Stir the chicken into the sauce and beans in the pan. Return to the fryer and reheat for 2 minutes.

Chicken Pasta Pie

Servings: 4
Cooking Time: 40 Minutes
Ingredients:
- 1/3 cup green bell peppers, diced
- ¼ cup yellow bell peppers, diced
- ½ cup mozzarella cheese, grated
- 3/4 cup grated Parmesan cheese
- 2/3 cup ricotta cheese
- 2 tbsp butter, melted
- 1 egg
- ¼ tsp salt
- 6 oz cooked spaghetti
- 2 tsp olive oil
- 1/3 cup diced onions
- 2 cloves minced garlic
- ¼ lb ground chicken
- 1 cup marinara sauce
- ½ tsp dried oregano

Directions:

1. Combine the ricotta cheese, 1 tbsp of Parmesan cheese, minced garlic, and salt in a bowl. Whisk the melted butter and egg in another bowl. Add the remaining Parmesan cheese and cooked spaghetti and mix well. Set aside. Warm the olive oil in a skillet over medium heat. Add in onions, green bell peppers, yellow bell peppers and cook for 3 minutes until the onions tender. Stir in ground chicken and cook for 5 minutes until no longer pink.

2. Preheat air fryer at 350ºF. Press spaghetti mixture into a greased baking pan, then spread ricotta mixture on top, and finally top with the topping mixture, followed by the marinara sauce. Place baking pan in the frying basket and Bake for 10 minutes. Scatter with mozzarella cheese on top and cook for 4 more minutes. Let rest for 20 minutes before releasing the sides of the baking pan. Cut into slices and serve sprinkled with oregano.

Turkey Scotch Eggs

Servings: 4
Cooking Time: 30 Minutes
Ingredients:

- 1 ½ lb ground turkey
- 1 tbsp ground cumin
- 1 tsp ground coriander
- 2 garlic cloves, minced
- 3 raw eggs
- 1 ½ cups bread crumbs
- 6 hard-cooked eggs, peeled
- ½ cup flour

Directions:

1. Preheat air fryer to 370°F. Place the ground turkey, cumin, coriander, garlic, one egg, and ½ cup of bread crumbs in a large bowl and mix until well incorporated.
2. Divide into 6 equal portions, then flatten each into long ovals. Set aside. In a shallow bowl, beat the remaining raw eggs. In another shallow bowl, add flour. Do the same with another plate for bread crumbs. Roll each cooked egg in flour, then wrap with one oval of chicken sausage until completely covered.
3. Roll again in flour, then coat in the beaten egg before rolling in bread crumbs. Arrange the eggs in the greased frying basket. Air Fry for 12-14 minutes, flipping once until the sausage is cooked and the eggs are brown. Serve.

Garlic Chicken

Servings: 4
Cooking Time: 30 Minutes
Ingredients:

- 4 bone-in skinless chicken thighs
- 1 tbsp olive oil
- 1 tbsp lemon juice
- 3 tbsp cornstarch
- 1 tsp dried sage
- Black pepper to taste
- 20 garlic cloves, unpeeled

Directions:

1. Preheat air fryer to 370°F. Brush the chicken with olive oil and lemon juice, then drizzle cornstarch, sage, and pepper.Put the chicken in the frying basket and scatter the garlic cloves on top. Roast for 25 minutes or until the garlic is soft, and the chicken is cooked through. Serve.

Enchilada Chicken Quesadillas

Servings: 4

Cooking Time: 35 Minutes

Ingredients:

- 2 cups cooked chicken breasts, shredded
- 1 can diced green chilies, including juice
- 2 cups grated Mexican cheese blend
- 3/4 cup sour cream
- 2 tsp chili powder
- 1 tsp cumin
- 1 tbsp chipotle sauce
- 1 tsp dried onion flakes
- ½ tsp salt
- 3 tbsp butter, melted
- 8 flour tortillas

Directions:

1. In a small bowl, whisk the sour cream, chipotle sauce and chili powder. Let chill in the fridge until ready to use.

2. Preheat air fryer at 350ºF. Mix the chicken, green chilies, cumin, and salt in a bowl. Set aside. Brush on one side of a tortilla lightly with melted butter. Layer with ¼ cup of chicken, onion flakes and ¼ cup of Mexican cheese. Top with a second tortilla and lightly brush with butter on top. Repeat with the remaining ingredients. Place quesadillas, butter side down, in the frying basket and Bake for 3 minutes. Cut them into 6 sections and serve with cream sauce on the side.

Saucy Chicken Thighs

Servings: 4

Cooking Time: 35 Minutes

Ingredients:

- 8 boneless, skinless chicken thighs
- 1 tbsp Italian seasoning
- Salt and pepper to taste
- 2 garlic cloves, minced
- ½ tsp apple cider vinegar
- ½ cup honey
- ¼ cup Dijon mustard

Directions:

1. Preheat air fryer to 400°F. Season the chicken with Italian seasoning, salt, and black pepper. Place in the greased frying basket and Bake for 15 minutes, flipping once halfway through cooking.

2. While the chicken is cooking, add garlic, honey, vinegar, and Dijon mustard in a saucepan and stir-fry over medium heat for 4 minutes or until the sauce has thickened and warmed through. Transfer the thighs to a serving dish and drizzle with honey-mustard sauce. Serve and enjoy!

Chicken Tikka

Servings: 4
Cooking Time: 15 Minutes

Ingredients:

- ¼ cup plain Greek yogurt
- 1 clove garlic, minced
- 1 tablespoon ketchup
- 1 tablespoon extra-virgin olive oil
- 1 tablespoon lemon juice
- ½ teaspoon salt
- ½ teaspoon ground cumin
- ½ teaspoon paprika
- ¼ teaspoon ground cinnamon
- ½ teaspoon ground black pepper
- ½ teaspoon cayenne pepper
- 1 pound boneless, skinless chicken thighs

Directions:

1. In a large bowl, stir together the yogurt, garlic, ketchup, olive oil, lemon juice, salt, cumin, paprika, cinnamon, black pepper, and cayenne pepper until combined.

2. Add the chicken thighs to the bow and fold the yogurt-spice mixture over the chicken thighs until they're covered with the marinade. Cover with plastic wrap and place in the refrigerator for 30 minutes.

3. When ready to cook the chicken, remove from the refrigerator and preheat the air fryer to 370°F.

4. Liberally spray the air fryer basket with olive oil mist. Place the chicken thighs into the air fryer basket, leaving space between the thighs to turn.

5. Cook for 10 minutes, turn the chicken thighs, and cook another 5 minutes (or until the internal temperature reaches 165°F).

6. Remove the chicken from the air fryer and serve warm with desired sides.

Beef，pork & Lamb Recipes

Original Köttbullar

Servings: 4
Cooking Time: 30 Minutes

Ingredients:

- 1 lb ground beef
- 1 small onion, chopped
- 1 clove garlic, minced
- 1/3 cup bread crumbs
- 1 egg, beaten
- Salt and pepper to taste
- 1 cup beef broth
- 1/3 cup heavy cream
- 2 tbsp flour

Directions:

1. Preheat air fryer to 370°F. Combine beef, onion, garlic, crumbs, egg, salt and pepper in a bowl. Scoop 2 tbsp of mixture and form meatballs with hands. Place the meatballs in the greased frying basket. Bake for 14 minutes.

2. Meanwhile, stir-fry beef broth and heavy cream in a saucepan over medium heat for 2 minutes; stir in flour. Cover and simmer for 4 minutes or until the sauce thicken. Transfer meatballs to a serving dish and drizzle with sauce. Serve and enjoy!

Sloppy Joes

Servings: 4

Cooking Time: 17 Minutes

Ingredients:

- oil for misting or cooking spray
- 1 pound very lean ground beef
- 1 teaspoon onion powder
- ⅓ cup ketchup
- ¼ cup water
- ½ teaspoon celery seed
- 1 tablespoon lemon juice
- 1½ teaspoons brown sugar
- 1¼ teaspoons low-sodium Worcestershire sauce
- ½ teaspoon salt (optional)
- ½ teaspoon vinegar
- ⅛ teaspoon dry mustard
- hamburger or slider buns

Directions:

1. Spray air fryer basket with nonstick cooking spray or olive oil.
2. Break raw ground beef into small chunks and pile into basket.
3. Cook at 390°F for 5minutes. Stir to break apart and cook 3minutes. Stir and cook 4 minutes longer or until meat is well done.
4. Remove meat from air fryer, drain, and use a knife and fork to crumble into small pieces.
5. Give your air fryer basket a quick rinse to remove any bits of meat.
6. Place all the remaining ingredients except the buns in a 6 x 6-inch baking pan and mix together.
7. Add meat and stir well.
8. Cook at 330°F for 5minutes. Stir and cook for 2minutes.
9. Scoop onto buns.

Better-than-chinese-take-out Pork Ribs

Servings: 3

Cooking Time: 35 Minutes

Ingredients:

- 1½ tablespoons Hoisin sauce (see here; gluten-free, if a concern)
- 1½ tablespoons Regular or low-sodium soy sauce or gluten-free tamari sauce
- 1½ tablespoons Shaoxing (Chinese cooking rice wine), dry sherry, or white grape juice
- 1½ teaspoons Minced garlic
- ¾ teaspoon Ground dried ginger
- ¾ teaspoon Ground white pepper
- 1½ pounds Pork baby back rib rack(s), cut into 2-bone pieces

Directions:

1. Mix the hoisin sauce, soy or tamari sauce, Shaoxing or its substitute, garlic, ginger, and white pepper in a large bowl. Add the rib sections and stir well to coat. Cover and refrigerate for at least 2 hours or up to 24 hours, stirring the rib sections in the marinade occasionally.
2. Preheat the air fryer to 350°F . Set the ribs in their bowl on the counter as the machine heats.
3. When the machine is at temperature, set the rib pieces on their sides in a single layer in the basket with as much air space between them as possible. Air-fry for 35 minutes, turning and rearranging the pieces once, until deeply browned and sizzling.
4. Use kitchen tongs to transfer the rib pieces to a large serving bowl or platter. Wait a minute or two before serving them so the meat can reabsorb some of its own juices.

Easy Tex-mex Chimichangas

Servings: 2

Cooking Time: 8 Minutes

Ingredients:

- ¼ pound Thinly sliced deli roast beef, chopped
- ½ cup (about 2 ounces) Shredded Cheddar cheese or shredded Tex-Mex cheese blend
- ¼ cup Jarred salsa verde or salsa rojo
- ½ teaspoon Ground cumin
- ½ teaspoon Dried oregano
- 2 Burrito-size (12-inch) flour tortilla(s), not corn tortillas (gluten-free, if a concern)
- ⅔ cup Canned refried beans
- Vegetable oil spray

Directions:

1. Preheat the air fryer to 375°F .

2. Stir the roast beef, cheese, salsa, cumin, and oregano in a bowl until well mixed.

3. Lay a tortilla on a clean, dry work surface. Spread ⅓ cup of the refried beans in the center lower third of the tortilla(s), leaving an inch on either side of the spread beans.

4. For one chimichanga, spread all of the roast beef mixture on top of the beans. For two, spread half of the roast beef mixture on each tortilla.

5. At either "end" of the filling mixture, fold the sides of the tortilla up and over the filling, partially covering it. Starting with the unfolded side of the tortilla just below the filling, roll the tortilla closed. Fold and roll the second filled tortilla, as necessary.

6. Coat the exterior of the tortilla(s) with vegetable oil spray. Set the chimichanga(s) seam side down in the basket, with at least ½ inch air space between them if you're working with two. Air-fry undisturbed for 8 minutes, or until the tortilla is lightly browned and crisp.

7. Use kitchen tongs to gently transfer the chimichanga(s) to a wire rack. Cool for at last 5 minutes or up to 20 minutes before serving.

Honey Pork Links

Servings:4

Cooking Time: 20 Minutes

Ingredients:

- 12 oz ground mild pork sausage, removed from casings
- 1 tsp rubbed sage
- 2 tbsp honey
- ⅛ tsp cayenne pepper
- ⅛ tsp paprika
- Salt and pepper to taste

Directions:

1. Preheat air fryer to 400ºF. Remove the sausage from the casings. Transfer to a bowl and add the remaining ingredients. Mix well. Make 8 links out of the mixture. Add the links to the frying basket and Air Fry for 8-10 minutes, flipping once. Serve right away.

Pretzel-coated Pork Tenderloin

Servings: 4
Cooking Time: 10 Minutes
Ingredients:

- 1 Large egg white(s)
- 2 teaspoons Dijon mustard (gluten-free, if a concern)
- 1½ cups (about 6 ounces) Crushed pretzel crumbs (see the headnote; gluten-free, if a concern)
- 1 pound (4 sections) Pork tenderloin, cut into ¼-pound (4-ounce) sections
- Vegetable oil spray

Directions:

1. Preheat the air fryer to 350°F .
2. Set up and fill two shallow soup plates or small pie plates on your counter: one for the egg white(s), whisked with the mustard until foamy; and one for the pretzel crumbs.
3. Dip a section of pork tenderloin in the egg white mixture and turn it to coat well, even on the ends. Let any excess egg white mixture slip back into the rest, then set the pork in the pretzel crumbs. Roll it several times, pressing gently, until the pork is evenly coated, even on the ends. Generously coat the pork section with vegetable oil spray, set it aside, and continue coating and spraying the remaining sections.
4. Set the pork sections in the basket with at least ¼ inch between them. Air-fry undisturbed for 10 minutes, or until an instant-read meat thermometer inserted into the center of one section registers 145°F.
5. Use kitchen tongs to transfer the pieces to a wire rack. Cool for 3 to 5 minutes before serving.

Beef & Spinach Sautée

Servings: 4
Cooking Time: 30 Minutes
Ingredients:

- 2 tomatoes, chopped
- 2 tbsp crumbled Goat cheese
- ½ lb ground beef
- 1 shallot, chopped
- 2 garlic cloves, minced
- 2 cups baby spinach
- 2 tbsp lemon juice
- 1/3 cup beef broth

Directions:

1. Preheat air fryer to 370°F. Crumble the beef in a baking pan and place it in the air fryer. Air Fry for 3-7 minutes, stirring once. Drain the meat and make sure it's browned. Toss in the tomatoes, shallot, and garlic and Air Fry for an additional 4-8 minutes until soft. Toss in the spinach, lemon juice, and beef broth and cook for 2-4 minutes until the spinach wilts. Top with goat cheese and serve.

Calzones South Of The Border

Servings: 8

Cooking Time: 8 Minutes

Ingredients:

- Filling
- ¼ pound ground pork sausage
- ½ teaspoon chile powder
- ¼ teaspoon ground cumin
- ⅛ teaspoon garlic powder
- ⅛ teaspoon onion powder
- ⅛ teaspoon oregano
- ½ cup ricotta cheese
- 1 ounce sharp Cheddar cheese, shredded
- 2 ounces Pepper Jack cheese, shredded
- 1 4-ounce can chopped green chiles, drained
- oil for misting or cooking spray
- salsa, sour cream, or guacamole
- Crust
- 2 cups white wheat flour, plus more for kneading and rolling
- 1 package (¼ ounce) RapidRise yeast
- 1 teaspoon salt
- ½ teaspoon chile powder
- ½ teaspoon ground cumin
- 1 cup warm water (115°F to 125°F)
- 2 teaspoons olive oil

Directions:

1. Crumble sausage into air fryer baking pan and stir in the filling seasonings: chile powder, cumin, garlic powder, onion powder, and oregano. Cook at 390°F for 2minutes. Stir, breaking apart, and cook for 3 to 4minutes, until well done. Remove and set aside on paper towels to drain.

2. To make dough, combine flour, yeast, salt, chile powder, and cumin. Stir in warm water and oil until soft dough forms. Turn out onto lightly floured board and knead for 3 or 4minutes. Let dough rest for 10minutes.

3. Place the three cheeses in a medium bowl. Add cooked sausage and chiles and stir until well mixed.

4. Cut dough into 8 pieces.

5. Working with 4 pieces of the dough, press each into a circle about 5 inches in diameter. Top each dough circle with 2 heaping tablespoons of filling. Fold over into a half-moon shape and press edges together. Seal edges firmly to prevent leakage. Spray both sides with oil or cooking spray.

6. Place 4 calzones in air fryer basket and cook at 360°F for 5minutes. Mist with oil or spray and cook for 3minutes, until crust is done and nicely browned.

7. While the first batch is cooking, press out the remaining dough, fill, and shape into calzones.

8. Spray both sides with oil or cooking spray and cook for 5minutes. If needed, mist with oil and continue cooking for 3 minutes longer. This second batch will cook a little faster than the first because your air fryer is already hot.

9. Serve plain or with salsa, sour cream, or guacamole.

Classic Salisbury Steak Burgers

Servings: 4
Cooking Time: 35 Minutes
Ingredients:
- ¼ cup bread crumbs
- 2 tbsp beef broth
- 1 tbsp cooking sherry
- 1 tbsp ketchup
- 1tbsp Dijon mustard
- 2 tsp Worcestershire sauce
- ½ tsp onion powder
- ½ tsp garlic powder
- 1 lb ground beef
- 1 cup sliced mushrooms
- 1 tbsp butter
- 4 buns, split and toasted

Directions:
1. Preheat the air fryer to 375°F. Combine the bread crumbs, broth, cooking sherry, ketchup, mustard, Worcestershire sauce, garlic and onion powder and mix well. Add the beef and mix with hands, then form into 4 patties and refrigerate while preparing the mushrooms. Mix the mushrooms and butter in a 6-inch pan. Place the pan in the air fryer and Bake for 8-10 minutes, stirring once until the mushrooms are brown and tender. Remove and set aside. Line the frying basket with round parchment paper and punch holes in it. Lay the burgers in a single layer and cook for 11-14 minutes or until cooked through. Put the burgers on the bun bottoms, top with the mushrooms, then the bun tops.

Cheesy Mushroom-stuffed Pork Loins

Servings:3
Cooking Time: 30 Minutes
Ingredients:
- ¾ cup diced mushrooms
- 2 tsp olive oil
- 1 shallot, diced
- Salt and pepper to taste
- 3 center-cut pork loins
- 6 Gruyère cheese slices

Directions:
1. Warm the olive oil in a skillet over medium heat. Add in shallot and mushrooms and stir-fry for 3 minutes. Sprinkle with salt and pepper and cook for 1 minute.
2. Preheat air fryer to 350ºF. Cut a pocket into each pork loin and set aside. Stuff an even amount of mushroom mixture into each chop pocket and top with 2 Gruyere cheese slices into each pocket. Place the pork in the lightly greased frying basket and Air Fry for 11 minutes cooked through and the cheese has melted. Let sit onto a cutting board for 5 minutes before serving.

Blackberry Bbq Glazed Country-style Ribs

Servings: 2

Cooking Time: 40 Minutes

Ingredients:

- ½ cup + 2 tablespoons sherry or Madeira wine, divided
- 1 pound boneless country-style pork ribs
- salt and freshly ground black pepper
- 1 tablespoon Chinese 5-spice powder
- ¼ cup blackberry preserves
- ¼ cup hoisin sauce*
- 1 clove garlic, minced
- 1 generous tablespoon grated fresh ginger
- 2 scallions, chopped
- 1 tablespoon sesame seeds, toasted

Directions:

1. Preheat the air fryer to 330°F and pour ½ cup of the sherry into the bottom of the air fryer drawer.
2. Season the ribs with salt, pepper and the 5-spice powder.
3. Air-fry the ribs at 330°F for 20 minutes, turning them over halfway through the cooking time.
4. While the ribs are cooking, make the sauce. Combine the remaining sherry, blackberry preserves, hoisin sauce, garlic and ginger in a small saucepan. Bring to a simmer on the stovetop for a few minutes, until the sauce thickens.
5. When the time is up on the air fryer, turn the ribs over, pour a little sauce on the ribs and air-fry for another 10 minutes at 330°F. Turn the ribs over again, pour on more of the sauce and air-fry at 330°F for a final 10 minutes.
6. Let the ribs rest for at least 5 minutes before serving them warm with a little more glaze brushed on and the scallions and sesame seeds sprinkled on top.

Italian Meatballs

Servings: 4

Cooking Time: 12 Minutes

Ingredients:

- 12 ounces lean ground beef
- 4 ounces Italian sausage, casing removed
- ½ cup breadcrumbs
- 1 cup grated Parmesan cheese
- 1 egg
- 2 tablespoons milk
- 2 teaspoons Italian seasoning
- ½ teaspoon onion powder
- ½ teaspoon garlic powder
- Pinch of red pepper flakes

Directions:

1. In a large bowl, place all the ingredients and mix well. Roll out 24 meatballs.
2. Preheat the air fryer to 360°F.
3. Place the meatballs in the air fryer basket and cook for 12 minutes, tossing every 4 minutes. Using a food thermometer, check to ensure the internal temperature of the meatballs is 165°F.

Premium Steakhouse Salad

Servings:2

Cooking Time: 20 Minutes

Ingredients:

- 1 head iceberg lettuce, cut into thin strips
- 2 tbsp olive oil
- 1 tbsp white wine vinegar
- 1 tbsp Greek yogurt
- 1 tsp Dijon mustard
- 1 (¾-lb) strip steak
- Salt and pepper to taste
- 2 tbsp chopped walnuts
- ¼ cup blue cheese crumbles
- 4 cherry tomatoes, halved
- 4 fig wedges

Directions:

1. In a bowl, whisk the olive oil, vinegar, Greek yogurt, and mustard. Let chill covered in the fridge until ready to use. Preheat air fryer to 400ºF. Sprinkle the steak with salt and pepper. Place it in the greased frying basket and Air Fry for 9 minutes or until you reach your desired doneness, flipping once. Let sit onto a cutting board for 5 minutes.

2. Combine lettuce and mustard dressing in a large bowl, then divide between 2 medium bowls. Thinly slice steak and add to salads. Scatter with walnuts, blue cheese, cherry tomatoes, and fig wedges. Serve immediately.

Boneless Ribeyes

Servings: 2

Cooking Time: 10-15 Minutes

Ingredients:

- 2 8-ounce boneless ribeye steaks
- 4 teaspoons Worcestershire sauce
- ½ teaspoon garlic powder
- pepper
- 4 teaspoons extra virgin olive oil
- salt

Directions:

1. Season steaks on both sides with Worcestershire sauce. Use the back of a spoon to spread evenly.
2. Sprinkle both sides of steaks with garlic powder and coarsely ground black pepper to taste.
3. Drizzle both sides of steaks with olive oil, again using the back of a spoon to spread evenly over surfaces.
4. Allow steaks to marinate for 30minutes.
5. Place both steaks in air fryer basket and cook at 390°F for 5minutes.
6. Turn steaks over and cook until done:
7. Medium rare: additional 5 minutes
8. Medium: additional 7 minutes
9. Well done: additional 10 minutes
10. Remove steaks from air fryer basket and let sit 5minutes. Salt to taste and serve.

French-style Steak Salad

Servings: 4
Cooking Time: 25 Minutes
Ingredients:

- 1 cup sliced strawberries
- 4 tbsp crumbled blue cheese
- ¼ cup olive oil
- Salt and pepper to taste
- 1 flank steak
- ¼cup balsamic vinaigrette
- 1 tbsp Dijon mustard
- 2 tbsp lemon juice
- 8 cups baby arugula
- ½ red onion, sliced
- 4 tbsp pecan pieces
- 4 tbsp sunflower seeds
- 1 sliced kiwi
- 1 sliced orange

Directions:

1. In a bowl, whisk olive oil, salt, lemon juice and pepper. Toss in flank steak and let marinate covered in the fridge for 30 minutes up to overnight. Preheat air fryer at 325ºF. Place flank steak in the greased frying basket and Bake for 18-20 minutes until rare, flipping once. Let rest for 5 minutes before slicing thinly against the grain.

2. In a salad bowl, whisk balsamic vinaigrette and mustard. Stir in arugula, salt, and pepper. Divide between 4 serving bowls. Top each salad with blue cheese, onion, pecan, sunflower seeds, strawberries, kiwi, orange and sliced steak. Serve immediately.

Bbq Back Ribs

Servings: 4
Cooking Time: 40 Minutes
Ingredients:

- 2 tbsp light brown sugar
- Salt and pepper to taste
- 2 tsp onion powder
- 1 tsp garlic powder
- 1 tsp mustard powder
- 1 tsp dried marjoram
- ½ tsp smoked paprika
- 1 tsp cayenne pepper
- 1 ½ pounds baby back ribs
- 2 tbsp barbecue sauce

Directions:

1. Preheat the air fryer to 375°F. Combine the brown sugar, salt, pepper, onion and garlic powder, mustard, paprika, cayenne, and marjoram in a bowl and mix. Pour into a small glass jar. Brush the ribs with barbecue sauce and sprinkle 1 tbsp of the seasoning mix. Rub the seasoning all over the meat. Set the ribs in the greased frying basket. Bake for 25 minutes until nicely browned, flipping them once halfway through cooking. Serve hot!

Teriyaki Country-style Pork Ribs

Servings: 3

Cooking Time: 30 Minutes

Ingredients:

- 3 tablespoons Regular or low-sodium soy sauce or gluten-free tamari sauce
- 3 tablespoons Honey
- ¾ teaspoon Ground dried ginger
- ¾ teaspoon Garlic powder
- 3 8-ounce boneless country-style pork ribs
- Vegetable oil spray

Directions:

1. Preheat the air fryer to 350°F .

2. Mix the soy or tamari sauce, honey, ground ginger, and garlic powder in another bowl until uniform

3. Smear about half of this teriyaki sauce over all sides of the country-style ribs. Reserve the remainder of the teriyaki sauce. Generously coat the meat with vegetable oil spray.

4. When the machine is at temperature, place the country-style ribs in the basket with as much air space between them as possible. Air-fry undisturbed for 15 minutes. Turn the country-style ribs (but keep the space between them) and brush them all over with the remaining teriyaki sauce. Continue air-frying undisturbed for 15 minutes, or until an instant-read meat thermometer inserted into the center of one rib registers at least 145°F.

5. Use kitchen tongs to transfer the country-style ribs to a wire rack. Cool for 5 minutes before serving.

Crispy Pierogi With Kielbasa And Onions

Servings: 3

Cooking Time: 20 Minutes

Ingredients:

- 6 Frozen potato and cheese pierogi, thawed (about 12 pierogi to 1 pound)
- ½ pound Smoked kielbasa, sliced into ½-inch-thick rounds
- ¾ cup Very roughly chopped sweet onion, preferably Vidalia
- Vegetable oil spray

Directions:

1. Preheat the air fryer to 375°F .

2. Put the pierogi, kielbasa rounds, and onion in a large bowl. Coat them with vegetable oil spray, toss well, spray again, and toss until everything is glistening.

3. When the machine is at temperature, dump the contents of the bowl it into the basket. (Items may be leaning against each other and even on top of each other.) Air-fry, tossing and rearranging everything twice so that all covered surfaces get exposed, for 20 minutes, or until the sausages have begun to brown and the pierogi are crisp.

4. Pour the contents of the basket onto a serving platter. Wait a minute or two just to take make sure nothing's searing hot before serving.

Tamari-seasoned Pork Strips

Servings:4
Cooking Time: 40 Minutes
Ingredients:

- 3 tbsp olive oil
- 2 tbsp tamari
- 2 tsp red chili paste
- 2 tsp yellow mustard
- 2 tsp granulated sugar
- 1 lb pork shoulder strips
- 1 cup white rice, cooked
- 6 scallions, chopped
- ½ tsp garlic powder
- 1 tbsp lemon juice
- 1 tsp lemon zest
- ½ tsp salt

Directions:

1. Add 2 tbsp of olive oil, tamari, chili paste, mustard, and sugar to a bowl and whisk until everything is well mixed. Set aside half of the marinade. Toss pork strips in the remaining marinade and put in the fridge for 30 minutes.

2. Preheat air fryer to 350ºF. Place the pork strips in the frying basket and Air Fry for 16-18 minutes, tossing once. Transfer cooked pork to the bowl along with the remaining marinade and toss to coat. Set aside. In a medium bowl, stir in the cooked rice, garlic, lemon juice, lemon zest, and salt and cover. Spread on a serving plate. Arrange the pork strips over and top with scallions. Serve.

Homemade Pork Gyoza

Servings: 4
Cooking Time: 50 Minutes
Ingredients:

- 8 wonton wrappers
- 4 oz ground pork, browned
- 1 green apple
- 1 tsp rice vinegar
- 1 tbsp vegetable oil
- ½ tbsp oyster sauce
- 1 tbsp soy sauce
- A pinch of white pepper

Directions:

1. Preheat air fryer to 350ºF. Combine the oyster sauce, soy sauce, rice vinegar, and white pepper in a small bowl. Add in the pork and stir thoroughly. Peel and core the apple, and slice into small cubes. Add the apples to the meat mixture, and combine thoroughly. Divide the filling between the wonton wrappers. Wrap the wontons into triangles and seal with a bit of water. Brush the wrappers with vegetable oil. Place them in the greased frying basket. Bake for 25 minutes until crispy golden brown on the outside and juicy and delicious on the inside. Serve.

Fish And Seafood Recipes

Spiced Salmon Croquettes

Servings: 6
Cooking Time: 20 Minutes
Ingredients:
- 1 can Alaskan pink salmon, bones removed
- 1 lime, zested
- 1 red chili, minced
- 2 tbsp cilantro, chopped
- 1 egg, beaten
- ½ cup bread crumbs
- 2 scallions, diced
- 1 tsp garlic powder
- Salt and pepper to taste

Directions:
1. Preheat air fryer to 400°F. Mix salmon, beaten egg, bread crumbs and scallions in a large bowl. Add garlic, lime, red chili, cilantro, salt and pepper. Divide into 6 even portions and shape into patties. Place them in the greased frying basket and Air Fry for 7 minutes. Flip them and cook for 4 minutes or until golden. Serve.

Caribbean Skewers

Servings: 4
Cooking Time: 25 Minutes
Ingredients:
- 1 ½ lb large shrimp, peeled and deveined
- 1 can pineapple chunks, drained, liquid reserved
- 1 red bell pepper, chopped
- 3 scallions, chopped
- 1 tbsp lemon juice
- 1 tbsp olive oil
- ½ tsp jerk seasoning
- ⅛ tsp cayenne pepper
- 2 tbsp cilantro, chopped

Directions:
1. Preheat the air fryer to 37-°F. Thread the shrimp, pineapple, bell pepper, and scallions onto 8 bamboo skewers. Mix 3 tbsp of pineapple juice with lemon juice, olive oil, jerk seasoning, and cayenne pepper. Brush every bit of the mix over the skewers. Place 4 kebabs in the frying basket, add a rack, and put the rest of the skewers on top. Bake for 6-9 minutes and rearrange at about 4-5 minutes. Cook until the shrimp curl and pinken. Sprinkle with freshly chopped cilantro and serve.

Sweet & Spicy Swordfish Kebabs

Servings: 4

Cooking Time: 30 Minutes

Ingredients:

- ½ cup canned pineapple chunks, drained, juice reserved
- 1 lb swordfish steaks, cubed
- ½ cup large red grapes
- 1 tbsp honey
- 2 tsp grated fresh ginger
- 1 tsp olive oil
- Pinch cayenne pepper

Directions:

1. Preheat air fryer to 370°F. Poke 8 bamboo skewers through the swordfish, pineapple, and grapes. Mix the honey, 1 tbsp of pineapple juice, ginger, olive oil, and cayenne in a bowl, then use a brush to rub the mix on the kebabs. Allow the marinate to sit on the kebab for 10 minutes. Grill the kebabs for 8-12 minutes until the fish is cooked through and the fruit is soft and glazed. Brush the kebabs again with the mix, then toss the rest of the marinade. Serve warm and enjoy!

Summer Sea Scallops

Servings: 4

Cooking Time: 30 Minutes

Ingredients:

- 1 cup asparagus
- 1 cup peas
- 1 cup chopped broccoli
- 2 tsp olive oil
- ½ tsp dried oregano
- 12 oz sea scallops

Directions:

1. Preheat air fryer to 400°F. Add the asparagus, peas, and broccoli to a bowl and mix with olive oil. Put the bowl in the fryer and Air Fry for 4-6 minutes until crispy and soft. Take the veggies out and add the herbs; let sit. Add the scallops to the fryer and Air Fry for 4-5 minutes until the scallops are springy to the touch. Serve immediately with the vegetables. Enjoy!

Crispy Fish Sandwiches

Servings: 4
Cooking Time: 25 Minutes
Ingredients:

- ½ cup torn iceberg lettuce
- ½ cup mayonnaise
- 1 tbsp Dijon mustard
- ½ cup diced dill pickles
- 1 tsp capers
- 1 tsp tarragon
- 1 tsp dill
- Salt and pepper to taste
- 1/3 cup flour
- 2 tbsp cornstarch
- 1 tsp smoked paprika
- ¼ cup milk
- 1 egg
- ½ cup bread crumbs
- 4 cod fillets, cut in half
- 1 vine-ripe tomato, sliced
- 4 hamburger buns

Directions:

1. Mix the mayonnaise, mustard, pickles, capers, tarragon, dill, salt, and pepper in a small bowl and let the resulting tartare sauce chill covered in the fridge until ready to use. Preheat air fryer at 375ºF. In a bowl, mix the flour, cornstarch, paprika, and salt. In another bowl, beat the milk and egg and in a third bowl, add the breadcrumbs. Roll the cod in the flour mixture, shake off excess flour. Then, dip in the egg, shake off excess egg. Finally, dredge in the breadcrumbs mixture. Place fish pieces in the greased frying basket and Air Fry for 6 minutes, flipping once. Add cooked fish, lettuce, tomato slices, and tartar sauce to each bottom bun and top with the top bun. Serve.

Basil Crab Cakes With Fresh Salad

Servings:2
Cooking Time: 25 Minutes
Ingredients:

- 8 oz lump crabmeat
- 2 tbsp mayonnaise
- ½ tsp Dijon mustard
- ½ tsp lemon juice
- ½ tsp lemon zest
- 2 tsp minced yellow onion
- ¼ tsp prepared horseradish
- ¼ cup flour
- ¼ cup pine nuts
- 2 lemon wedges
- 1 egg white, beaten
- 1 tbsp basil, minced
- 1 tbsp olive oil
- 2 tsp white wine vinegar
- Salt and pepper to taste
- 4 oz arugula
- ½ cup blackberries

Directions:

1. Preheat air fryer to 400ºF. Combine the crabmeat, mayonnaise, mustard, lemon juice and zest, onion, horseradish, flour, egg white, and basil in a bowl. Form mixture into 4 patties. Place the patties in the lightly greased frying basket and Air Fry for 10 minutes, flipping once. Combine olive oil, vinegar, salt, and pepper in a bowl. Toss in the arugula and share into 2 medium bowls. Add 2 crab cakes to each bowl and scatter with blackberries, pine nuts, and lemon wedges. Serve warm.

Lemon-dill Salmon Burgers

Servings: 4

Cooking Time: 8 Minutes

Ingredients:

- 2 (6-ounce) fillets of salmon, finely chopped by hand or in a food processor
- 1 cup fine breadcrumbs
- 1 teaspoon freshly grated lemon zest
- 2 tablespoons chopped fresh dill weed
- 1 teaspoon salt
- freshly ground black pepper
- 2 eggs, lightly beaten
- 4 brioche or hamburger buns
- lettuce, tomato, red onion, avocado, mayonnaise or mustard, to serve

Directions:

1. Preheat the air fryer to 400°F.

2. Combine all the ingredients in a bowl. Mix together well and divide into four balls. Flatten the balls into patties, making an indentation in the center of each patty with your thumb (this will help the burger stay flat as it cooks) and flattening the sides of the burgers so that they fit nicely into the air fryer basket.

3. Transfer the burgers to the air fryer basket and air-fry for 4 minutes. Flip the burgers over and air-fry for another 3 to 4 minutes, until nicely browned and firm to the touch.

4. Serve on soft brioche buns with your choice of topping – lettuce, tomato, red onion, avocado, mayonnaise or mustard.

Mom's Tuna Melt Toastie

Servings: 4

Cooking Time: 30 Minutes

Ingredients:

- 4 white bread slices
- 2 oz canned tuna
- 2 tbsp mayonnaise
- ½ lemon, zested and juiced
- Salt and pepper to taste
- ½ red onion, finely sliced
- 1 red tomato, sliced
- 4 cheddar cheese slices
- 2 tbsp butter, melted

Directions:

1. Preheat air fryer to 360°F. Put the butter-greased bread slices in the frying basket. Toast for 6 minutes. Meanwhile, mix the tuna, lemon juice and zest, salt, pepper, and mayonnaise in a small bowl. When the time is over, slide the frying basket out, flip the bread slices, and spread the tuna mixture evenly all over them. Cover with tomato slices, red onion, and cheddar cheese. Toast for 10 minutes or until the cheese is melted and lightly bubbling. Serve and enjoy!

Caribbean Jerk Cod Fillets

Servings:2
Cooking Time: 20 Minutes
Ingredients:

- ¼ cup chopped cooked shrimp
- ¼ cup diced mango
- 1 tomato, diced
- 2 tbsp diced red onion
- 1 tbsp chopped parsley
- ¼ tsp ginger powder
- 2 tsp lime juice
- Salt and pepper to taste
- 2 cod fillets
- 2 tsp Jerk seasoning

Directions:

1. In a bowl, combine the shrimp, mango, tomato, red onion, parsley, ginger powder, lime juice, salt, and black pepper. Let chill the salsa in the fridge until ready to use.

2. Preheat air fryer to 350ºF. Sprinkle cod fillets with Jerk seasoning. Place them in the greased frying basket and Air Fry for 10 minutes or until the cod is opaque and flakes easily with a fork. Divide between 2 medium plates. Serve topped with the Caribbean salsa.

Lemon-dill Salmon With Green Beans

Servings: 4
Cooking Time: 20 Minutes
Ingredients:

- 20 halved cherry tomatoes
- 4 tbsp butter
- 4 garlic cloves, minced
- ¼ cup chopped dill
- Salt and pepper to taste
- 4 wild-caught salmon fillets
- ¼ cup white wine
- 1 lemon, thinly sliced
- 1 lb green beans, trimmed
- 2 tbsp chopped parsley

Directions:

1. Preheat air fryer to 390°F. Combine butter, garlic, dill, wine, salt, and pepper in a small bowl. Spread the seasoned butter over the top of the salmon. Arrange the fish in a single layer in the frying basket. Top with ½ of the lemon slices and surround the fish with green beans and tomatoes. Bake for 12-15 minutes until salmon is cooked and vegetables are tender. Top with parsley and serve with lemon slices on the side.

Potato Chip-crusted Cod

Servings: 2
Cooking Time: 20 Minutes
Ingredients:

- ½ cup crushed potato chips
- 1 tsp chopped tarragon
- 1/8 tsp salt
- 1 tsp cayenne powder
- 1 tbsp Dijon mustard
- ¼ cup buttermilk
- 1 tsp lemon juice
- 1 tbsp butter, melted
- 2 cod fillets

Directions:

1. Preheat air fryer at 350ºF. Mix all ingredients in a bowl. Press potato chip mixture evenly across tops of cod. Place cod fillets in the greased frying basket and Air Fry for 10 minutes until the fish is opaque and flakes easily with a fork. Serve immediately.

Baltimore Crab Cakes

Servings: 4
Cooking Time: 35 Minutes
Ingredients:

- ½ lb lump crabmeat, shells discarded
- 2 tbsp mayonnaise
- ½ tsp yellow mustard
- ½ tsp lemon juice
- ½ tbsp minced shallot
- ¼ cup bread crumbs
- 1 egg
- Salt and pepper to taste
- 4 poached eggs
- ½ cup bechamel sauce
- 2 tsp chopped chives
- 1 lemon, cut into wedges

Directions:

1. Preheat air fryer at 400ºF. Combine all ingredients, except eggs, sauce, and chives, in a bowl. Form mixture into 4 patties. Place crab cakes in the greased frying basket and Air Fry for 10 minutes, flipping once. Transfer them to a serving dish. Top each crab cake with 1 poached egg, drizzle with Bechamel sauce and scatter with chives and lemon wedges. Serve and enjoy!

Kid´s Flounder Fingers

Servings: 4
Cooking Time: 45 Minutes
Ingredients:

- 1 lb catfish flounder fillets, cut into 1-inch chunks
- ½ cup seasoned fish fry breading mix

Directions:

1. Preheat air fryer to 400°F. In a resealable bag, add flounder and breading mix. Seal bag and shake until the fish is coated. Place the nuggets in the greased frying basket and Air Fry for 18-20 minutes, shaking the basket once until crisp. Serve warm and enjoy!

Speedy Shrimp Paella

Servings: 4

Cooking Time: 20 Minutes

Ingredients:

- 2 cups cooked rice
- 1 red bell pepper, chopped
- ¼ cup vegetable broth
- ½ tsp turmeric
- ½ tsp dried thyme
- 1 cup cooked small shrimp
- ½ cup baby peas
- 1 tomato, diced

Directions:

1. Preheat air fryer to 340°F. Gently combine rice, red bell pepper, broth, turmeric, and thyme in a baking pan. Bake in the air fryer until the rice is hot, about 9 minutes. Remove the pan from the air fryer and gently stir in shrimp, peas, and tomato. Return to the air fryer and cook until bubbling and all ingredients are hot, 5-8 minutes. Serve and enjoy!

The Best Shrimp Risotto

Servings: 4

Cooking Time: 50 Minutes + 5 Minutes To Sit

Ingredients:

- 1/3 cup grated Parmesan
- 2 tbsp olive oil
- 1 lb peeled shrimp, deveined
- 1 onion, chopped
- 1 red bell pepper, chopped
- Salt and pepper to taste
- 1 cup Carnaroli rice
- 21/3 cups vegetable stock
- 2 tbsp butter
- 1 tbsp heavy cream

Directions:

1. Preheat the air fryer to 380°F. Add a tbsp of olive oil to a cake pan, then toss in the shrimp. Put the pan in the frying basket and cook the shrimp for 4-7 minutes or until they curl and pinken. Remove the shrimp and set aside. Add the other tbsp of olive oil to the cake pan, then add the onion, bell pepper, salt, and pepper and Air Fry for 3 minutes. Add the rice to the cake pan, stir, and cook for 2 minutes. Add the stock, stir again, and cover the pan with foil. Bake for another 18-22 minutes, stirring twice until the rice is tender. Remove the foil. Return the shrimp to the pan along with butter, heavy cream, and Parmesan, then cook for another minute. Stir and serve.

Flounder Fillets

Servings: 4
Cooking Time: 8 Minutes

Ingredients:

- 1 egg white
- 1 tablespoon water
- 1 cup panko breadcrumbs
- 2 tablespoons extra-light virgin olive oil
- 4 4-ounce flounder fillets
- salt and pepper
- oil for misting or cooking spray

Directions:

1. Preheat air fryer to 390°F.
2. Beat together egg white and water in shallow dish.
3. In another shallow dish, mix panko crumbs and oil until well combined and crumbly (best done by hand).
4. Season flounder fillets with salt and pepper to taste. Dip each fillet into egg mixture and then roll in panko crumbs, pressing in crumbs so that fish is nicely coated.
5. Spray air fryer basket with nonstick cooking spray and add fillets. Cook at 390°F for 3minutes.
6. Spray fish fillets but do not turn. Cook 5 minutes longer or until golden brown and crispy. Using a spatula, carefully remove fish from basket and serve.

Fish Piccata With Crispy Potatoes

Servings: 4
Cooking Time: 30 Minutes

Ingredients:

- 4 cod fillets
- 1 tbsp butter
- 2 tsp capers
- 1 garlic clove, minced
- 2 tbsp lemon juice
- ½ lb asparagus, trimmed
- 2 large potatoes, cubed
- 1 tbsp olive oil
- Salt and pepper to taste
- ¼ tsp garlic powder
- 1 tsp dried rosemary
- 1 tsp dried parsley
- 1 tsp chopped dill

Directions:

1. Preheat air fryer to 380°F. Place each fillet on a large piece of foil. Top each fillet with butter, capers, dill, garlic, and lemon juice. Fold the foil over the fish and seal the edges to make a pouch. Mix asparagus, parsley, potatoes, olive oil, salt, rosemary, garlic powder, and pepper in a large bowl. Place asparagus in the frying basket. Roast for 4 minutes, then shake the basket. Top vegetable with foil packets and Roast for another 8 minutes. Turn off air fryer and let it stand for 5 minutes. Serve warm and enjoy.

Crunchy And Buttery Cod With Ritz® Cracker Crust

Servings: 2

Cooking Time: 10 Minutes

Ingredients:

- 4 tablespoons butter, melted
- 8 to 10 RITZ® crackers, crushed into crumbs
- 2 (6-ounce) cod fillets
- salt and freshly ground black pepper
- 1 lemon

Directions:

1. Preheat the air fryer to 380°F.
2. Melt the butter in a small saucepan on the stovetop or in a microwavable dish in the microwave, and then transfer the butter to a shallow dish. Place the crushed RITZ® crackers into a second shallow dish.
3. Season the fish fillets with salt and freshly ground black pepper. Dip them into the butter and then coat both sides with the RITZ® crackers.
4. Place the fish into the air fryer basket and air-fry at 380°F for 10 minutes, flipping the fish over halfway through the cooking time.
5. Serve with a wedge of lemon to squeeze over the top.

Sriracha Salmon Melt Sandwiches

Servings: 4

Cooking Time: 20 Minutes

Ingredients:

- 2 tbsp butter, softened
- 2 cans pink salmon
- 2 English muffins
- 1/3 cup mayonnaise
- 2 tbsp Dijon mustard
- 1 tbsp fresh lemon juice
- 1/3 cup chopped celery
- ½ tsp sriracha sauce
- 4 slices tomato
- 4 slices Swiss cheese

Directions:

1. Preheat the air fryer to 370°F. Split the English muffins with a fork and spread butter on the 4 halves. Put the halves in the basket and Bake for 3-5 minutes, or until toasted. Remove and set aside. Combine the salmon, mayonnaise, mustard, lemon juice, celery, and sriracha in a bowl. Divide among the English muffin halves. Top each sandwich with tomato and cheese and put in the frying basket. Bake for 4-6 minutes or until the cheese is melted and starts to brown. Serve hot.

Garlic-butter Lobster Tails

Servings:2
Cooking Time: 20 Minutes
Ingredients:

- 2 lobster tails
- 1 tbsp butter, melted
- ½ tsp Old Bay Seasoning
- ½ tsp garlic powder
- 1 tbsp chopped parsley
- 2 lemon wedges

Directions:

1. Preheat air fryer to 400ºF. Using kitchen shears, cut down the middle of each lobster tail on the softer side. Carefully run your finger between the lobster meat and the shell to loosen the meat. Place lobster tails in the frying basket, cut sides up, and Air Fry for 4 minutes. Rub with butter, garlic powder and Old Bay seasoning and cook for 4 more minutes. Garnish with parsley and lemon wedges. Serve and enjoy!

Vegetable Side Dishes Recipes

Mexican-style Frittata

Servings: 4
Cooking Time: 35 Minutes
Ingredients:

- ½ cup shredded Cotija cheese
- ½ cup cooked black beans
- 1 cooked potato, sliced
- 3 eggs, beaten
- Salt and pepper to taste

Directions:

1. Preheat air fryer to 350°F. Mix the eggs, beans, half of Cotija cheese, salt, and pepper in a bowl. Pour the mixture into a greased baking dish. Top with potato slices. Place the baking dish in the frying basket and Air Fry for 10 minutes. Slide the basket out and sprinkle the remaining Cotija cheese over the dish. Cook for 10 more minutes or until golden and bubbling. Slice into wedges to serve.

Southwestern Sweet Potato Wedges

Servings: 4
Cooking Time: 30 Minutes
Ingredients:

- 2 sweet potatoes, peeled and cut into ½-inch wedges
- 2 tsp olive oil
- 2 tbsp cornstarch
- 1 tsp garlic powder
- ¼ tsp ground allspice
- ¼ tsp paprika
- ⅛ tsp cayenne pepper

Directions:

1. Preheat air fryer to 400°F. Place the sweet potatoes in a bowl. Add some olive oil and toss to coat, then transfer to the frying basket. Roast for 8 minutes. Sprinkle the potatoes with cornstarch, garlic powder, allspice, paprika, and cayenne, then toss. Put the potatoes back into the fryer and Roast for 12-17 more minutes. Shake the basket a couple of times while cooking. The potatoes should be golden and crispy. Serve warm.

Roasted Cauliflower With Garlic And Capers

Servings: 3

Cooking Time: 10 Minutes

Ingredients:

- 3 cups (about 15 ounces) 1-inch cauliflower florets
- 2 tablespoons Olive oil
- 1½ tablespoons Drained and rinsed capers, chopped
- 2 teaspoons Minced garlic
- ¼ teaspoon Table salt
- Up to ¼ teaspoon Red pepper flakes

Directions:

1. Preheat the air fryer to 375°F
2. Stir the cauliflower florets, olive oil, capers, garlic, salt, and red pepper flakes in a large bowl until the florets are evenly coated.
3. When the machine is at temperature, put the florets in the basket, spreading them out to as close to one layer as you can. Air-fry for 10 minutes, tossing once to get any covered pieces exposed to the air currents, until tender and lightly browned.
4. Dump the contents of the basket into a serving bowl or onto a serving platter. Cool for a minute or two before serving.

Perfect Asparagus

Servings: 3

Cooking Time: 10 Minutes

Ingredients:

- 1 pound Very thin asparagus spears
- 2 tablespoons Olive oil
- 1 teaspoon Coarse sea salt or kosher salt
- ¾ teaspoon Finely grated lemon zest

Directions:

1. Preheat the air fryer to 400°F.
2. Trim just enough off the bottom of the asparagus spears so they'll fit in the basket. Put the spears on a large plate and drizzle them with some of the olive oil. Turn them over and drizzle more olive oil, working to get all the spears coated.
3. When the machine is at temperature, place the spears in one direction in the basket. They may be touching. Air-fry for 10 minutes, tossing and rearranging the spears twice, until tender.
4. Dump the contents of the basket on a serving platter. Spread out the spears. Sprinkle them with the salt and lemon zest while still warm. Serve at once.

Fried Cauliflowerwith Parmesan Lemon Dressing

Servings: 2

Cooking Time: 12 Minutes

Ingredients:

- 4 cups cauliflower florets (about half a large head)
- 1 tablespoon olive oil
- salt and freshly ground black pepper
- 1 teaspoon finely chopped lemon zest
- 1 tablespoon fresh lemon juice (about half a lemon)
- ¼ cup grated Parmigiano-Reggiano cheese
- 4 tablespoons extra virgin olive oil
- ¼ teaspoon salt
- lots of freshly ground black pepper
- 1 tablespoon chopped fresh parsley

Directions:

1. Preheat the air fryer to 400°F.
2. Toss the cauliflower florets with the olive oil, salt and freshly ground black pepper. Air-fry for 12 minutes, shaking the basket a couple of times during the cooking process.
3. While the cauliflower is frying, make the dressing. Combine the lemon zest, lemon juice, Parmigiano-Reggiano cheese and olive oil in a small bowl. Season with salt and lots of freshly ground black pepper. Stir in the parsley.
4. Turn the fried cauliflower out onto a serving platter and drizzle the dressing over the top.

Mashed Sweet Potato Tots

Servings: 18

Cooking Time: 12 Minutes

Ingredients:

- 1 cup cooked mashed sweet potatoes
- 1 egg white, beaten
- ⅛ teaspoon ground cinnamon
- 1 dash nutmeg
- 2 tablespoons chopped pecans
- 1½ teaspoons honey
- salt
- ½ cup panko breadcrumbs
- oil for misting or cooking spray

Directions:

1. Preheat air fryer to 390°F.
2. In a large bowl, mix together the potatoes, egg white, cinnamon, nutmeg, pecans, honey, and salt to taste.
3. Place panko crumbs on a sheet of wax paper.
4. For each tot, use about 2 teaspoons of sweet potato mixture. To shape, drop the measure of potato mixture onto panko crumbs and push crumbs up and around potatoes to coat edges. Then turn tot over to coat other side with crumbs.
5. Mist tots with oil or cooking spray and place in air fryer basket in single layer.
6. Cook at 390°F for 12 minutes, until browned and crispy.
7. Repeat steps 5 and 6 to cook remaining tots.

Sage & Thyme Potatoes

Servings: 4

Cooking Time: 30 Minutes

Ingredients:

- 2 red potatoes, peeled and cubed
- ¼ cup olive oil
- 1 tsp dried sage
- ½ tsp dried thyme
- ½ tsp salt
- 2 tbsp grated Parmesan

Directions:

1. Preheat air fryer to 360°F. Coat the red potatoes with olive oil, sage, thyme and salt in a bowl. Pour the potatoes into the air frying basket and Roast for 10 minutes. Stir the potatoes and sprinkle the Parmesan over the top. Continue roasting for 8 more minutes. Serve hot.

Crispy Brussels Sprouts

Servings: 3

Cooking Time: 12 Minutes

Ingredients:

- 1¼ pounds Medium, 2-inch-in-length Brussels sprouts
- 1½ tablespoons Olive oil
- ¾ teaspoon Table salt

Directions:

1. Preheat the air fryer to 400°F.
2. Halve each Brussels sprout through the stem end, pulling off and discarding any discolored outer leaves. Put the sprout halves in a large bowl, add the oil and salt, and stir well to coat evenly, until the Brussels sprouts are glistening.
3. When the machine is at temperature, scrape the contents of the bowl into the basket, gently spreading the Brussels sprout halves into as close to one layer as possible. Air-fry for 12 minutes, gently tossing and rearranging the vegetables twice to get all covered or touching parts exposed to the air currents, until crisp and browned at the edges.
4. Gently pour the contents of the basket onto a wire rack. Cool for a minute or two before serving.

Cinnamon Roasted Pumpkin

Servings: 2

Cooking Time: 25 Minutes

Ingredients:

- 1 lb pumpkin, halved crosswise and seeded
- 1 tsp coconut oil
- 1 tsp sugar
- ½ tsp ground nutmeg
- 1 tsp ground cinnamon

Directions:

1. Prepare the pumpkin by rubbing coconut oil on the cut sides. In a small bowl, combine sugar, nutmeg and cinnamon. Sprinkle over the pumpkin. Preheat air fryer to 325°F. Put the pumpkin in the greased frying basket, cut sides up. Bake until the squash is soft in the center, 15 minutes. Test with a knife to ensure softness. Serve.

Succulent Roasted Peppers

Servings:2

Cooking Time: 35 Minutes

Ingredients:

- 2 red bell peppers
- 2 tbsp olive oil
- Salt to taste
- 1 tsp dill, chopped

Directions:

1. Preheat air fryer to 400ºF. Remove the tops and bottoms of the peppers. Cut along rib sections and discard the seeds. Combine the bell peppers and olive oil in a bowl. Place bell peppers in the frying basket. Roast for 24 minutes, flipping once. Transfer the roasted peppers to a small bowl and cover for 15 minutes. Then, peel and discard the skins. Sprinkle with salt and dill and serve.

Salmon Salad With Steamboat Dressing

Servings: 4

Cooking Time: 18 Minutes

Ingredients:

- ¼ teaspoon salt
- 1½ teaspoons dried dill weed
- 1 tablespoon fresh lemon juice
- 8 ounces fresh or frozen salmon fillet (skin on)
- 8 cups shredded romaine, Boston, or other leaf lettuce
- 8 spears cooked asparagus, cut in 1-inch pieces
- 8 cherry tomatoes, halved or quartered

Directions:

1. Mix the salt and dill weed together. Rub the lemon juice over the salmon on both sides and sprinkle the dill and salt all over. Refrigerate for 15 to 20minutes.

2. Make Steamboat Dressing and refrigerate while cooking salmon and preparing salad.

3. Cook salmon in air fryer basket at 330°F for 18 minutes. Cooking time will vary depending on thickness of fillets. When done, salmon should flake with fork but still be moist and tender.

4. Remove salmon from air fryer and cool slightly. At this point, the skin should slide off easily. Cut salmon into 4 pieces and discard skin.

5. Divide the lettuce among 4 plates. Scatter asparagus spears and tomato pieces evenly over the lettuce, allowing roughly 2 whole spears and 2 whole cherry tomatoes per plate.

6. Top each salad with one portion of the salmon and drizzle with a tablespoon of dressing. Serve with additional dressing to pass at the table.

Tofu & Broccoli Salad

Servings: 4
Cooking Time: 17 Minutes
Ingredients:
- Broccoli Salad
- 4 cups fresh broccoli, cut into bite-size pieces
- ½ cup red onion, chopped
- ⅓ cup raisins or dried cherries
- ¾ cup sliced almonds
- ½ cup Asian-style salad dressing
- Tofu
- 4 ounces extra firm tofu
- 1 teaspoon smoked paprika
- 1 teaspoon onion powder
- ¼ teaspoon salt
- 2 tablespoons cornstarch
- 1 tablespoon extra virgin olive oil

Directions:
1. Place several folded paper towels on a plate and set tofu on top. Cover tofu with another folded paper towel, put another plate on top, and add heavy items such as canned goods to weigh it down. Press tofu for 30minutes.
2. While tofu is draining, combine all salad ingredients in a large bowl. Toss together well, cover, and chill until ready to serve.
3. Cut the tofu into small cubes, about ¼-inch thick. Sprinkle the cubes top and bottom with the paprika, onion powder, and salt.
4. Place cornstarch in small plastic bag, add tofu, and shake until cubes are well coated.
5. Place olive oil in another small plastic bag, add coated tofu, and shake to coat well.
6. Cook at 330°F for 17 minutes or until as crispy as you like.
7. To serve, stir chilled salad well, divide among 4 plates, and top with fried tofu.

Mouth-watering Provençal Mushrooms

Servings: 4
Cooking Time: 35 Minutes
Ingredients:
- 2 lb mushrooms, quartered
- 2-3 tbsp olive oil
- ½ tsp garlic powder
- 2 tsp herbs de Provence
- 2 tbsp dry white wine

Directions:
1. Preheat air fryer to 320°F. Beat together the olive oil, garlic powder, herbs de Provence, and white wine in a bowl. Add the mushrooms and toss gently to coat. Spoon the mixture onto the frying basket and Bake for 16-18 minutes, stirring twice. Serve hot and enjoy!

Cheesy Potato Pot

Servings: 4

Cooking Time: 13 Minutes

Ingredients:

- 3 cups cubed red potatoes (unpeeled, cut into ½-inch cubes)
- ½ teaspoon garlic powder
- salt and pepper
- 1 tablespoon oil
- chopped chives for garnish (optional)
- Sauce
- 2 tablespoons milk
- 1 tablespoon butter
- 2 ounces sharp Cheddar cheese, grated
- 1 tablespoon sour cream

Directions:

1. Place potato cubes in large bowl and sprinkle with garlic, salt, and pepper. Add oil and stir to coat well.
2. Cook at 390°F for 13 minutes or until potatoes are tender. Stir every 4 or 5minutes during cooking time.
3. While potatoes are cooking, combine milk and butter in a small saucepan. Warm over medium-low heat to melt butter. Add cheese and stir until it melts. The melted cheese will remain separated from the milk mixture. Remove from heat until potatoes are done.
4. When ready to serve, add sour cream to cheese mixture and stir over medium-low heat just until warmed. Place cooked potatoes in serving bowl. Pour sauce over potatoes and stir to combine.
5. Garnish with chives if desired.

Speedy Baked Caprese With Avocado

Servings:4

Cooking Time: 15 Minutes

Ingredients:

- 4 oz fresh mozzarella
- 8 cherry tomatoes
- 2 tsp olive oil
- 2 halved avocados, pitted
- ¼ tsp salt
- 2 tbsp basil, torn

Directions:

1. Preheat air fryer to 375ºF. In a bowl, combine tomatoes and olive oil. Set aside. Add avocado halves, cut sides up, in the frying basket, scatter tomatoes around halves, and Bake for 7 minutes. Divide avocado halves between 4 small plates, top each with 2 tomatoes and sprinkle with salt. Cut mozzarella cheese and evenly distribute over tomatoes. Scatter with the basil to serve.

Garlic-parmesan Popcorn

Servings: 2

Cooking Time: 15 Minutes

Ingredients:

- 2 tsp grated Parmesan cheese
- ¼ cup popcorn kernels
- 1 tbsp lemon juice
- 1 tsp garlic powder

Directions:

1. Preheat air fryer to 400°F. Line the basket with aluminum foil. Put the popcorn kernels in a single layer and Grill for 6-8 minutes until they stop popping. Remove them into a bowl. Drizzle with lemon juice and toss until well coated. Sprinkle with garlic powder and grated Parmesan and toss to coat. Drizzle with more lemon juice. Serve.

Crispy Cauliflower Puffs

Servings: 12

Cooking Time: 9 Minutes

Ingredients:

- 1½ cups Riced cauliflower
- 1 cup (about 4 ounces) Shredded Monterey Jack cheese
- ¾ cup Seasoned Italian-style panko bread crumbs (gluten-free, if a concern)
- 2 tablespoons plus 1 teaspoon All-purpose flour or potato starch
- 2 tablespoons plus 1 teaspoon Vegetable oil
- 1 plus 1 large yolk Large egg(s)
- ¾ teaspoon Table salt
- Vegetable oil spray

Directions:

1. Preheat the air fryer to 375°F .

2. Stir the riced cauliflower, cheese, bread crumbs, flour or potato starch, oil, egg(s) and egg yolk (if necessary), and salt in a large bowl to make a thick batter.

3. Using 2 tablespoons of the batter, form a compact ball between your clean, dry palms. Set it aside and continue forming more balls: 7 more for a small batch, 11 more for a medium batch, or 15 more for a large batch.

4. Generously coat the balls on all sides with vegetable oil spray. Set them in the basket with as much air space between them as possible. Air-fry undisturbed for 7 minutes, or until golden brown and crisp. If the machine is at 360°F, you may need to add 2 minutes to the cooking time.

5. Gently pour the contents of the basket onto a wire rack. Cool the puffs for 5 minutes before serving.

Perfect Broccoli

Servings: 4
Cooking Time: 12 Minutes
Ingredients:

- 5 cups (about 1 pound 10 ounces) 1- to 1½-inch fresh broccoli florets (not frozen)
- Olive oil spray
- ¾ teaspoon Table salt

Directions:

1. Preheat the air fryer to 375°F .
2. Put the broccoli florets in a big bowl, coat them generously with olive oil spray, then toss to coat all surfaces, even down into the crannies, spraying them in a couple of times more. Sprinkle the salt on top and toss again.
3. When the machine is at temperature, pour the florets into the basket. Air-fry for 10 minutes, tossing and rearranging the pieces twice so that all the covered or touching bits are eventually exposed to the air currents, until lightly browned but still crunchy. (If the machine is at 360°F, you may have to add 2 minutes to the cooking time.)
4. Pour the florets into a serving bowl. Cool for a minute or two, then serve hot.

Corn On The Cob

Servings: 4
Cooking Time: 12 Minutes
Ingredients:

- 2 large ears fresh corn
- olive oil for misting
- salt (optional)

Directions:

1. Shuck corn, remove silks, and wash.
2. Cut or break each ear in half crosswise.
3. Spray corn with olive oil.
4. Cook at 390°F for 12 minutes or until browned as much as you like.
5. Serve plain or with coarsely ground salt.

Sicilian Arancini

Servings: 4
Cooking Time: 20 Minutes
Ingredients:

- 1/3 minced red bell pepper
- 4 tsp grated Parmesan cheese
- 1 ¼ cup cooked rice
- 1 egg
- 3 tbsp plain flour
- 1/3 cup finely grated carrots
- 2 tbsp minced fresh parsley
- 2 tsp olive oil

Directions:

1. Preheat air fryer to 380°F. Add the rice, egg, and flour to a bowl and mix well. Add the carrots, bell peppers, parsley, and Parmesan cheese and mix again. Shape into 8 fritters. Brush with olive oil and place the fritters in the frying basket. Air Fry for 8-10 minutes, turning once, until golden. Serve hot and enjoy!

Vegetarians Recipes

Home-style Cinnamon Rolls

Servings: 4

Cooking Time: 40 Minutes

Ingredients:

- ½ pizza dough
- 1/3 cup dark brown sugar
- ¼ cup butter, softened
- ½ tsp ground cinnamon

Directions:

1. Preheat air fryer to 360°F. Roll out the dough into a rectangle. Using a knife, spread the brown sugar and butter, covering all the edges, and sprinkle with cinnamon.Fold the long side of the dough into a log, then cut it into 8 equal pieces, avoiding compression. Place the rolls, spiral-side up, onto a parchment-lined sheet. Let rise for 20 minutes. Grease the rolls with cooking spray and Bake for 8 minutes until golden brown. Serve right away.

Sweet & Spicy Vegetable Stir-fry

Servings: 2

Cooking Time: 45 Minutes

Ingredients:

- ½ pineapple, cut into bite-size chunks
- ¼ cup Tabasco sauce
- ¼ cup lime juice
- 2 tsp allspice
- 5 oz cauliflower florets
- 1 carrot, thinly sliced
- 1 cup frozen peas, thawed
- 2 scallions, chopped

Directions:

1. Preheat air fryer to 400°F. Whisk Tabasco sauce, lime juice, and allspice in a bowl. Then toss in cauliflower, pineapple, and carrots until coated. Strain the remaining sauce; reserve it. Air Fry the veggies for 12 minutes, shake, and Air Fry for 10-12 more minutes until cooked. Once the veggies are ready, remove to a bowl. Combine peas, scallions, and reserved sauce until coated. Transfer to a pan and Air Fry them for 3 minutes. Remove them to the bowl and serve right away.

Golden Fried Tofu

Servings: 4

Cooking Time: 20 Minutes

Ingredients:

- ¼ cup flour
- ¼ cup cornstarch
- 1 tsp garlic powder
- ¼ tsp onion powder
- Salt and pepper to taste
- 1 firm tofu, cubed
- 2 tbsp cilantro, chopped

Directions:

1. Preheat air fryer to 390°F. Combine the flour, cornstarch, salt, garlic, onion powder, and black pepper in a bowl. Stir well. Place the tofu cubes in the flour mix. Toss to coat. Spray the tofu with oil and place them in a single layer in the greased frying basket. Air Fry for 14-16 minutes, flipping the pieces once until golden and crunchy. Top with freshly chopped cilantro and serve immediately.

Cheese & Bean Burgers

Servings: 2
Cooking Time: 35 Minutes
Ingredients:

- 1 cup cooked black beans
- ½ cup shredded cheddar
- 1 egg, beaten
- Salt and pepper to taste
- 1 cup bread crumbs
- ½ cup grated carrots

Directions:

1. Preheat air fryer to 350°F. Mash the beans with a fork in a bowl. Mix in the cheese, salt, and pepper until evenly combined. Stir in half of the bread crumbs and egg. Shape the mixture into 2 patties. Coat each patty with the remaining bread crumbs and spray with cooking oil. Air Fry for 14-16 minutes, turning once. When ready, removeto a plate. Top with grated carrots and serve.

Green Bean & Baby Potato Mix

Servings: 4
Cooking Time: 25 Minutes
Ingredients:

- 1 lb baby potatoes, halved
- 4 garlic cloves, minced
- 2 tbsp olive oil
- Salt and pepper to taste
- ½ tsp hot paprika
- ½ tbsp taco seasoning
- 1 tbsp chopped parsley
- ½ lb green beans, trimmed

Directions:

1. Preheat air fryer to 375°F. Toss potatoes, garlic, olive oil, salt, pepper, hot paprika, and taco seasoning in a large bowl. Arrange the potatoes in a single layer in the air fryer basket. Air Fry for 10 minutes, then stir in green beans. Air Fry for another 10 minutes. Serve hot sprinkled with parsley.

Pinto Taquitos

Servings: 4
Cooking Time: 8 Minutes
Ingredients:

- 12 corn tortillas (6- to 7-inch size)
- Filling
- ½ cup refried pinto beans
- ½ cup grated sharp Cheddar or Pepper Jack cheese
- ¼ cup corn kernels (if frozen, measure after thawing and draining)
- 2 tablespoons chopped green onion
- 2 tablespoons chopped jalapeño pepper (seeds and ribs removed before chopping)
- ½ teaspoon lime juice
- ½ teaspoon chile powder, plus extra for dusting
- ½ teaspoon cumin
- ½ teaspoon garlic powder
- oil for misting or cooking spray
- salsa, sour cream, or guacamole for dipping

Directions:

1. Mix together all filling Ingredients.
2. Warm refrigerated tortillas for easier rolling. (Wrap in damp paper towels and microwave for 30 to 60 seconds.)
3. Working with one at a time, place 1 tablespoon of filling on tortilla and roll up. Spray with oil or cooking spray and dust outside with chile powder to taste.
4. Place 6 taquitos in air fryer basket (4 on bottom layer, 2 stacked crosswise on top). Cook at 390°F for 8 minutes, until crispy and brown.
5. Repeat step 4 to cook remaining taquitos.
6. Serve plain or with salsa, sour cream, or guacamole for dipping.

Chili Tofu & Quinoa Bowls

Servings: 2
Cooking Time: 30 Minutes
Ingredients:

- 1 cup diced peeled sweet potatoes
- ¼ cup chopped mixed bell peppers
- 1/8 cup sprouted green lentils
- ½ onion, sliced
- 1 tsp avocado oil
- 1/8 cup chopped carrots
- 8 oz extra-firm tofu, cubed
- ½ tsp smoked paprika
- ½ tsp chili powder
- ¼ tsp salt
- 2 tsp lime zest
- 1 cup cooked quinoa
- 2 lime wedges

Directions:

1. Preheat air fryer at 350°F. Combine the onion, carrots, bell peppers, green lentils, sweet potato, and avocado oil in a bowl. In another bowl, mix the tofu, paprika, chili powder, and salt. Add veggie mixture to the frying basket and Air Fry for 8 minutes. Stir in tofu mixture and cook for 8 more minutes. Combine lime zest and quinoa. Divide into 2 serving bowls. Top each with the tofu mixture and squeeze a lime wedge over. Serve warm.

Vegetarian Shepherd´s Pie

Servings: 4
Cooking Time: 40 Minutes
Ingredients:

- 1 russet potato, peeled and diced
- 1 tbsp olive oil
- 2 tbsp balsamic vinegar
- ¼ cup cheddar shreds
- 2 tbsp milk
- Salt and pepper to taste
- 2 tsp avocado oil
- 1 cup beefless grounds
- ½ onion, diced
- 3 cloves garlic
- 1 carrot, diced
- ¼ diced green bell peppers
- 1 celery stalk, diced
- 2/3 cup tomato sauce
- 1 tsp chopped rosemary
- 1 tbsp sesame seeds
- 1 tsp thyme leaves
- 1 lemon

Directions:

1. Add salted water to a pot over high heat and bring it to a boil. Add in diced potatoes and cook for 5 minutes until fork tender. Drain and transfer it to a bowl. Add in the olive oil cheddar shreds, milk, salt, and pepper and mash it until smooth. Set the potato topping aside.

2. Preheat air fryer at 350ºF. Place avocado oil, beefless grounds, garlic, onion, carrot, bell pepper, and celery in a skillet over medium heat and cook for 4 minutes until the veggies are tender. Stir in the remaining ingredients and turn the heat off. Spoon the filling into a greased cake pan. Top with the potato topping.

3. Using tines of a fork, create shallow lines along the top of mashed potatoes. Place cake pan in the frying basket and Bake for 12 minutes. Let rest for 10 minutes before serving sprinkled with sesame seeds and squeezed lemon.

Powerful Jackfruit Fritters

Servings:4
Cooking Time: 30 Minutes
Ingredients:

- 1 can jackfruit, chopped
- 1 egg, beaten
- 1 tbsp Dijon mustard
- 1 tbsp mayonnaise
- 1 tbsp prepared horseradish
- 2 tbsp grated yellow onion
- 2 tbsp chopped parsley
- 2 tbsp chopped nori
- 2 tbsp flour
- 1 tbsp Cajun seasoning
- ¼ tsp garlic powder
- ¼ tsp salt
- 2 lemon wedges

Directions:

1. In a bowl, combine jackfruit, egg, mustard, mayonnaise, horseradish, onion, parsley, nori, flour, Cajun seasoning, garlic, and salt. Let chill in the fridge for 15 minutes. Preheat air fryer to 350ºF. Divide the mixture into 12 balls. Place them in the frying basket and Air Fry for 10 minutes. Serve with lemon wedges.

Fake Shepherd´s Pie

Servings:6
Cooking Time: 40 Minutes
Ingredients:

- ½ head cauliflower, cut into florets
- 1 sweet potato, diced
- 1 tbsp olive oil
- ¼ cup cheddar shreds
- 2 tbsp milk
- Salt and pepper to taste
- 2 tsp avocado oil
- 1 cup beefless grounds

- ½ onion, diced
- 2 cloves garlic, minced
- 1 carrot, diced
- ½ cup green peas
- 1 stalk celery, diced
- 2/3 cup tomato sauce
- 1 tsp chopped rosemary
- 1 tsp thyme leaves

Directions:

1. Place cauliflower and sweet potato in a pot of salted boiling water over medium heat and simmer for 7 minutes until fork tender. Strain and transfer to a bowl. Put in avocado oil, cheddar, milk, salt and pepper. Mash until smooth.

2. Warm olive oil in a skillet over medium-high heat and stir in beefless grounds and vegetables and stir-fry for 4 minutes until veggies are tender. Stir in tomato sauce, rosemary, thyme, salt, and black pepper. Set aside.

3. Preheat air fryer to 350ºF. Spoon filling into a round cake pan lightly greased with olive oil and cover with the topping. Using the tines of a fork, run shallow lines in the top of cauliflower for a decorative touch. Place cake pan in the frying basket and Air Fry for 12 minutes. Let sit for 10 minutes before serving.

Roasted Vegetable Pita Pizza

Servings: 4
Cooking Time: 20 Minutes
Ingredients:

- 1 medium red bell pepper, seeded and cut into quarters
- 1 teaspoon extra-virgin olive oil
- ⅛ teaspoon black pepper
- ⅛ teaspoon salt
- Two 6-inch whole-grain pita breads
- 6 tablespoons pesto sauce
- ¼ small red onion, thinly sliced
- ½ cup shredded part-skim mozzarella cheese

Directions:

1. Preheat the air fryer to 400°F.
2. In a small bowl, toss the bell peppers with the olive oil, pepper, and salt.
3. Place the bell peppers in the air fryer and cook for 15 minutes, shaking every 5 minutes to prevent burning.
4. Remove the peppers and set aside. Turn the air fryer temperature down to 350°F.
5. Lay the pita bread on a flat surface. Cover each with half the pesto sauce; then top with even portions of the red bell peppers and onions. Sprinkle cheese over the top. Spray the air fryer basket with olive oil mist.
6. Carefully lift the pita bread into the air fryer basket with a spatula.
7. Cook for 5 to 8 minutes, or until the outer edges begin to brown and the cheese is melted.
8. Serve warm with desired sides.

Vegetable Hand Pies

Servings: 8
Cooking Time: 10 Minutes Per Batch
Ingredients:

- ¾ cup vegetable broth
- 8 ounces potatoes
- ¾ cup frozen chopped broccoli, thawed
- ¼ cup chopped mushrooms
- 1 tablespoon cornstarch
- 1 tablespoon milk
- 1 can organic flaky biscuits (8 large biscuits)
- oil for misting or cooking spray

Directions:

1. Place broth in medium saucepan over low heat.
2. While broth is heating, grate raw potato into a bowl of water to prevent browning. You will need ¾ cup grated potato.
3. Roughly chop the broccoli.
4. Drain potatoes and put them in the broth along with the broccoli and mushrooms. Cook on low for 5 minutes.
5. Dissolve cornstarch in milk, then stir the mixture into the broth. Cook about a minute, until mixture thickens a little. Remove from heat and cool slightly.
6. Separate each biscuit into 2 rounds. Divide vegetable mixture evenly over half the biscuit rounds, mounding filling in the center of each.
7. Top the four rounds with filling, then the other four rounds and crimp the edges together with a fork.
8. Spray both sides with oil or cooking spray and place 4 pies in a single layer in the air fryer basket.
9. Cook at 330°F for approximately 10 minutes.
10. Repeat with the remaining biscuits. The second batch may cook more quickly because the fryer will be hot.

Farfalle With White Sauce

Servings: 4
Cooking Time: 30 Minutes
Ingredients:

- 4 cups cauliflower florets
- 1 medium onion, chopped
- 8 oz farfalle pasta
- 2 tbsp chives, minced
- ½ cup cashew pieces
- 1 tbsp nutritional yeast
- 2 large garlic cloves, peeled
- 2 tbsp fresh lemon juice
- Salt and pepper to taste

Directions:

1. Preheat air fryer to 390°F. Put the cauliflower in the fryer, spray with oil, and Bake for 8 minutes. Remove the basket, stir, and add the onion. Roast for 10 minutes or until the cauliflower is golden and the onions soft. Cook the farfalle pasta according to the package directions. Set aside. Put the roasted cauliflower and onions along with the cashews, 1 ½ of cups water, yeast, garlic, lemon, salt, and pepper in a blender. Blend until creamy. Pour a large portion of the sauce on top of the warm pasta and add the minced scallions. Serve.

Cheesy Enchilada Stuffed Baked Potatoes

Servings: 4

Cooking Time: 37 Minutes

Ingredients:

- 2 medium russet potatoes, washed
- One 15-ounce can mild red enchilada sauce
- One 15-ounce can low-sodium black beans, rinsed and drained
- 1 teaspoon taco seasoning
- ½ cup shredded cheddar cheese
- 1 medium avocado, halved
- ½ teaspoon garlic powder
- ¼ teaspoon black pepper
- ¼ teaspoon salt
- 2 teaspoons fresh lime juice
- 2 tablespoon chopped red onion
- ¼ cup chopped cilantro

Directions:

1. Preheat the air fryer to 390°F.

2. Puncture the outer surface of the potatoes with a fork.

3. Set the potatoes inside the air fryer basket and cook for 20 minutes, rotate, and cook another 10 minutes.

4. In a large bowl, mix the enchilada sauce, black beans, and taco seasoning.

5. When the potatoes have finished cooking, carefully remove them from the air fryer basket and let cool for 5 minutes.

6. Using a pair of tongs to hold the potato if it's still too hot to touch, slice the potato in half lengthwise. Use a spoon to scoop out the potato flesh and add it into the bowl with the enchilada sauce. Mash the potatoes with the enchilada sauce mixture, creating a uniform stuffing.

7. Place the potato skins into an air-fryer-safe pan and stuff the halves with the enchilada stuffing. Sprinkle the cheese over the top of each potato.

8. Set the air fryer temperature to 350°F, return the pan to the air fryer basket, and cook for another 5 to 7 minutes to heat the potatoes and melt the cheese.

9. While the potatoes are cooking, take the avocado and scoop out the flesh into a small bowl. Mash it with the back of a fork; then mix in the garlic powder, pepper, salt, lime juice, and onion. Set aside.

10. When the potatoes have finished cooking, remove the pan from the air fryer and place the potato halves on a plate. Top with avocado mash and fresh cilantro. Serve immediately.

Authentic Mexican Esquites

Servings: 4
Cooking Time: 25 Minutes

Ingredients:

- 4 ears of corn, husk and silk removed
- 1 tbsp ground coriander
- 1 tbsp smoked paprika
- 1 tsp sea salt
- 1 tsp garlic powder
- 1 tsp onion powder
- 1 tsp dried lime peel
- 1 tsp cayenne pepper
- 3 tbsp mayonnaise
- 3 tbsp grated Cotija cheese
- 1 tbsp butter, melted
- 1 tsp epazote seasoning

Directions:

1. Preheat the air fryer to 400°F. Combine the coriander, paprika, salt, garlic powder, onion powder, lime peel, epazote and cayenne pepper in a small bowl and mix well. Pour into a small glass jar. Put the corn in the greased frying basket and Bake for 6-8 minutes or until the corn is crispy but tender. Make sure to rearrange the ears halfway through cooking.

2. While the corn is frying, combine the mayonnaise, cheese, and melted butter in a small bowl. Spread the mixture over the cooked corn, return to the fryer, and Bake for 3-5 minutes more or until the corn has brown spots. Remove from the fryer and sprinkle each cob with about ½ tsp of the spice mix.

Sweet Corn Bread

Servings: 6
Cooking Time: 35 Minutes

Ingredients:

- 2 eggs, beaten
- ½ cup cornmeal
- ½ cup pastry flour
- 1/3 cup sugar
- 1 tsp lemon zest
- ½ tbsp baking powder
- ¼ tsp salt
- ¼ tsp baking soda
- ½ tbsp lemon juice
- ½ cup milk
- ¼ cup sunflower oil

Directions:

1. Preheat air fryer to 350°F. Add the cornmeal, flour, sugar, lemon zest, baking powder, salt, and baking soda in a bowl. Stir with a whisk until combined. Add the eggs, lemon juice, milk, and oil to another bowl and stir well. Add the wet mixture to the dry mixture and stir gently until combined. Spray a baking pan with oil. Pour the batter in and Bake in the fryer for 25 minutes or until golden and a knife inserted in the center comes out clean. Cut into wedges and serve.

Vietnamese Gingered Tofu

Servings: 4
Cooking Time: 25 Minutes
Ingredients:
- 1 package extra-firm tofu, cubed
- 4 tsp shoyu
- 1 tsp onion powder
- ½ tsp garlic powder
- ½ tsp ginger powder
- ½ tsp turmeric powder
- Black pepper to taste
- 2 tbsp nutritional yeast
- 1 tsp dried rosemary
- 1 tsp dried dill
- 2 tsp cornstarch
- 2 tsp sunflower oil

Directions:
1. Sprinkle the tofu with shoyu and toss to coat. Add the onion, garlic, ginger, turmeric, and pepper. Gently toss to coat. Add the yeast, rosemary, dill, and cornstarch. Toss to coat. Dribble with the oil and toss again.
2. Preheat air fryer to 390°F. Spray the fryer basket with oil, put the tofu in the basket and Bake for 7 minutes. Remove, shake gently, and cook for another 7 minutes or until the tofu is crispy and golden. Serve warm.

Bite-sized Blooming Onions

Servings: 4
Cooking Time: 35 Minutes + Cooling Time
Ingredients:
- 1 lb cipollini onions
- 1 cup flour
- 1 tsp salt
- ½ tsp paprika
- 1 tsp cayenne pepper
- 2 eggs
- 2 tbsp milk

Directions:
1. Preheat the air fryer to 375°F. Carefully peel the onions and cut a ½ inch off the stem ends and trim the root ends. Place them root-side down on the cutting surface and cut the onions into quarters. Be careful not to cut al the way to the bottom. Cut each quarter into 2 sections and pull the wedges apart without breaking them.
2. In a shallow bowl, add the flour, salt, paprika, and cayenne, and in a separate shallow bowl, beat the eggs with the milk. Dip the onions in the flour, then dip in the egg mix, coating evenly, and then in the flour mix again. Shake off excess flour. Put the onions in the frying basket, cut-side up, and spray with cooking oil. Air Fry for 10-15 minutes until the onions are crispy on the outside, tender on the inside. Let cool for 10 minutes, then serve.

Two-cheese Grilled Sandwiches

Servings: 2

Cooking Time: 30 Minutes

Ingredients:

- 4 sourdough bread slices
- 2 cheddar cheese slices
- 2 Swiss cheese slices
- 1 tbsp butter
- 2 dill pickles, sliced

Directions:

1. Preheat air fryer to 360°F. Smear both sides of the sourdough bread with butter and place them in the frying basket. Toast the bread for 6 minutes, flipping once.

2. Divide the cheddar cheese between 2 of the bread slices. Cover the remaining 2 bread slices with Swiss cheese slices. Bake for 10 more minutes until the cheeses have melted and lightly bubbled and the bread has golden brown. Set the cheddar-covered bread slices on a serving plate, cover with pickles, and top each with the Swiss-covered slices. Serve and enjoy!

General Tso's Cauliflower

Servings: 4

Cooking Time: 15 Minutes

Ingredients:

- 1 head cauliflower cut into florets
- ¾ cup all-purpose flour, divided*
- 3 eggs, lightly beaten
- 1 cup panko breadcrumbs*
- canola or peanut oil, in a spray bottle
- 2 tablespoons oyster sauce
- ¼ cup soy sauce
- 2 teaspoons chili paste
- 2 tablespoons rice wine vinegar
- 2 tablespoons sugar
- ¼ cup water
- white or brown rice for serving
- steamed broccoli

Directions:

1. Set up dredging station using three bowls. Place the cauliflower in a large bowl and sprinkle ¼ cup of the flour over the top. Place the eggs in a second bowl and combine the panko breadcrumbs and remaining ½ cup flour in a third bowl. Toss the cauliflower in the flour to coat all the florets thoroughly. Dip the cauliflower florets in the eggs and finally toss them in the breadcrumbs to coat on all sides. Place the coated cauliflower florets on a baking sheet and spray generously with canola or peanut oil.

2. Preheat the air fryer to 400°F.

3. Air-fry the cauliflower at 400°F for 15 minutes, flipping the florets over for the last 3 minutes of the cooking process and spraying again with oil.

4. While the cauliflower is air-frying, make the General Tso Sauce. Combine the oyster sauce, soy sauce, chili paste, rice wine vinegar, sugar and water in a saucepan and bring the mixture to a boil on the stove top. Lower the heat and let it simmer for 10 minutes, stirring occasionally.

5. When the timer is up on the air fryer, transfer the cauliflower to a large bowl, pour the sauce over it all and toss to coat. Serve with white or brown rice and some steamed broccoli.

Desserts And Sweets

Easy Bread Pudding

Servings: 4
Cooking Time: 25 Minutes
Ingredients:
- 2 cups sandwich bread cubes
- ½ cup pecan pieces
- ½ cup raisins
- 3 eggs
- ¼ cup half-and-half
- ¼ cup dark corn syrup
- 1 tsp vanilla extract
- 2 tbsp bourbon
- 2 tbsp dark brown sugar
- ¼ tsp ground cinnamon
- ½ tsp nutmeg
- ¼ tsp salt

Directions:
1. Preheat air fryer at 325ºF. Spread the bread pieces in a cake pan and layer pecan pieces and raisins over the top. Whisk the eggs, half-and-half, corn syrup, bourbon, vanilla extract, sugar, cinnamon, nutmeg, and salt in a bowl. Pour egg mixture over pecan pieces. Let sit for 10 minutes. Place the cake pan in the frying basket and Bake for 15 minutes. Let cool onto a cooling rack for 10 minutes before slicing. Serve immediately.

Chocolate Macaroons

Servings: 16
Cooking Time: 8 Minutes
Ingredients:
- 2 Large egg white(s), at room temperature
- ⅛ teaspoon Table salt
- ½ cup Granulated white sugar
- 1½ cups Unsweetened shredded coconut
- 3 tablespoons Unsweetened cocoa powder

Directions:
1. Preheat the air fryer to 375°F .
2. Using an electric mixer at high speed, beat the egg white(s) and salt in a medium or large bowl until stiff peaks can be formed when the turned-off beaters are dipped into the mixture.
3. Still working with the mixer at high speed, beat in the sugar in a slow stream until the meringue is shiny and thick.
4. Scrape down and remove the beaters. Fold in the coconut and cocoa with a rubber spatula until well combined, working carefully to deflate the meringue as little as possible.
5. Scoop up 2 tablespoons of the mixture. Wet your clean hands and roll that little bit of coconut bliss into a ball. Set it aside and continue making more balls: 7 more for a small batch, 15 more for a medium batch, or 23 more for a large one.
6. Line the bottom of the machine's basket or the basket attachment with parchment paper. Set the balls on the parchment with as much air space between them as possible. Air-fry undisturbed for 8 minutes, or until dry, set, and lightly browned.
7. Use a nonstick-safe spatula to transfer the macaroons to a wire rack. Cool for at least 10 minutes before serving. Or cool to room temperature, about 30 minutes, then store in a sealed container at room temperature for up to 3 days.

Molten Chocolate Almond Cakes

Servings: 3

Cooking Time: 13 Minutes

Ingredients:

- butter and flour for the ramekins
- 4 ounces bittersweet chocolate, chopped
- ½ cup (1 stick) unsalted butter
- 2 eggs
- 2 egg yolks
- ¼ cup sugar
- ½ teaspoon pure vanilla extract, or almond extract
- 1 tablespoon all-purpose flour
- 3 tablespoons ground almonds
- 8 to 12 semisweet chocolate discs (or 4 chunks of chocolate)
- cocoa powder or powdered sugar, for dusting
- toasted almonds, coarsely chopped

Directions:

1. Butter and flour three (6-ounce) ramekins. (Butter the ramekins and then coat the butter with flour by shaking it around in the ramekin and dumping out any excess.)

2. Melt the chocolate and butter together, either in the microwave or in a double boiler. In a separate bowl, beat the eggs, egg yolks and sugar together until light and smooth. Add the vanilla extract. Whisk the chocolate mixture into the egg mixture. Stir in the flour and ground almonds.

3. Preheat the air fryer to 330°F.

4. Transfer the batter carefully to the buttered ramekins, filling halfway. Place two or three chocolate discs in the center of the batter and then fill the ramekins to ½-inch below the top with the remaining batter. Place the ramekins into the air fryer basket and air-fry at 330°F for 13 minutes. The sides of the cake should be set, but the centers should be slightly soft. Remove the ramekins from the air fryer and let the cakes sit for 5 minutes. (If you'd like the cake a little less molten, air-fry for 14 minutes and let the cakes sit for 4 minutes.)

5. Run a butter knife around the edge of the ramekins and invert the cakes onto a plate. Lift the ramekin off the plate slowly and carefully so that the cake doesn't break. Dust with cocoa powder or powdered sugar and serve with a scoop of ice cream and some coarsely chopped toasted almonds.

Fall Pumpkin Cake

Servings: 6

Cooking Time: 50 Minutes

Ingredients:

- 1/3 cup pecan pieces
- 5 gingersnap cookies
- 1/3 cup light brown sugar
- 6 tbsp butter, melted
- 3 eggs
- ½ tsp vanilla extract
- 1 cup pumpkin purée
- 2 tbsp sour cream
- ½ cup flour
- ¼ cup tapioca flour
- ½ tsp cornstarch
- ½ cup granulated sugar
- ½ tsp baking soda
- 1 tsp baking powder
- 1 tsp pumpkin pie spice
- 6 oz mascarpone cheese
- 1 1/3 cups powdered sugar
- 1 tsp cinnamon
- 2 tbsp butter, softened
- 1 tbsp milk
- 1 tbsp flaked almonds

Directions:

1. Blitz the pecans, gingersnap cookies, brown sugar, and 3 tbsp of melted butter in a food processor until combined. Press mixture into the bottom of a lightly greased cake pan. Preheat air fryer at 350ºF. In a bowl, whisk the eggs, remaining melted butter, ½ tsp of vanilla extract, pumpkin purée, and sour cream. In another bowl, combine the flour, tapioca flour, cornstarch, granulated sugar, baking soda, baking powder, and pumpkin pie spice. Add wet ingredients to dry ingredients and combine. Do not overmix. Pour the batter into a cake pan and cover it with aluminum foil. Place cake pan in the frying basket and Bake for 30 minutes. Remove the foil and cook for another 5 minutes. Let cool onto a cooling rack for 10 minutes. Then, turn cake onto a large serving platter. In a small bowl, whisk the mascarpone cheese, powdered sugar, remaining vanilla extract, cinnamon, softened butter, and milk. Spread over cooled cake and cut into slices. Serve sprinkled with almonds and enjoy!

Maple Cinnamon Cheesecake

Servings: 4

Cooking Time: 12 Minutes

Ingredients:

- 6 sheets of cinnamon graham crackers
- 2 tablespoons butter
- 8 ounces Neufchâtel cream cheese
- 3 tablespoons pure maple syrup
- 1 large egg
- ½ teaspoon ground cinnamon
- ¼ teaspoon salt

Directions:

1. Preheat the air fryer to 350°F.

2. Place the graham crackers in a food processor and process until crushed into a flour. Mix with the butter and press into a mini air-fryer-safe pan lined at the bottom with parchment paper. Place in the air fryer and cook for 4 minutes.

3. In a large bowl, place the cream cheese and maple syrup. Use a hand mixer or stand mixer and beat together until smooth. Add in the egg, cinnamon, and salt and mix on medium speed until combined.

4. Remove the graham cracker crust from the air fryer and pour the batter into the pan.

5. Place the pan back in the air fryer, adjusting the temperature to 315°F. Cook for 18 minutes. Carefully remove when cooking completes. The top should be lightly browned and firm.

6. Keep the cheesecake in the pan and place in the refrigerator for 3 or more hours to firm up before serving.

Sea-salted Caramel Cookie Cups

Servings: 12

Cooking Time: 12 Minutes

Ingredients:

- ⅓ cup butter
- ¼ cup brown sugar
- 1 teaspoon vanilla extract
- 1 large egg
- 1 cup all-purpose flour
- ½ cup old-fashioned oats
- ½ teaspoon baking soda
- ¼ teaspoon salt
- ⅓ cup sea-salted caramel chips

Directions:

1. Preheat the air fryer to 300°F.

2. In a large bowl, cream the butter with the brown sugar and vanilla. Whisk in the egg and set aside.

3. In a separate bowl, mix the flour, oats, baking soda, and salt. Then gently mix the dry ingredients into the wet. Fold in the caramel chips.

4. Divide the batter into 12 silicon muffin liners. Place the cookie cups into the air fryer basket and cook for 12 minutes or until a toothpick inserted in the center comes out clean.

5. Remove and let cool 5 minutes before serving.

Vanilla Butter Cake

Servings: 6
Cooking Time: 20-24 Minutes
Ingredients:

- ¾ cup plus 1 tablespoon All-purpose flour
- 1 teaspoon Baking powder
- ¼ teaspoon Table salt
- 8 tablespoons (½ cup/1 stick) Butter, at room temperature
- ½ cup Granulated white sugar
- 2 Large egg(s)
- 2 tablespoons Whole or low-fat milk (not fat-free)
- ¾ teaspoon Vanilla extract
- Baking spray (see here)

Directions:

1. Preheat the air fryer to 325°F (or 330°F, if that's the closest setting).
2. Mix the flour, baking powder, and salt in a small bowl until well combined.
3. Using an electric hand mixer at medium speed, beat the butter and sugar in a medium bowl until creamy and smooth, about 3 minutes, occasionally scraping down the inside of the bowl.
4. Beat in the egg or eggs, as well as the white or a yolk as necessary. Beat in the milk and vanilla until smooth. Turn off the beaters and add the flour mixture. Beat at low speed until thick and smooth.
5. Use the baking spray to generously coat the inside of a 6-inch round cake pan for a small batch, a 7-inch round cake pan for a medium batch, or an 8-inch round cake pan for a large batch. Scrape and spread the batter into the pan, smoothing the batter out to an even layer.
6. Set the pan in the basket and air-fry undisturbed for 20 minutes for a 6-inch layer, 22 minutes for a 7-inch layer, or 24 minutes for an 8-inch layer, or until a toothpick or cake tester inserted into the center of the cake comes out clean. Start checking it at the 15-minute mark to know where you are.
7. Use hot pads or silicone baking mitts to transfer the cake pan to a wire rack. Cool for 5 minutes. To unmold, set a cutting board over the baking pan and invert both the board and the pan. Lift the still-warm pan off the cake layer. Set the wire rack on top of the cake layer and invert all of it with the cutting board so that the cake layer is now right side up on the wire rack. Remove the cutting board and continue cooling the cake for at least 10 minutes or to room temperature, about 30 minutes, before slicing into wedges.

Donut Holes

Servings: 13
Cooking Time: 12 Minutes

Ingredients:

- 6 tablespoons Granulated white sugar
- 1½ tablespoons Butter, melted and cooled
- 2 tablespoons (or 1 small egg, well beaten) Pasteurized egg substitute, such as Egg Beaters
- 6 tablespoons Regular or low-fat sour cream (not fat-free)
- ¾ teaspoon Vanilla extract
- 1⅔ cups All-purpose flour
- ¾ teaspoon Baking powder
- ¼ teaspoon Table salt
- Vegetable oil spray

Directions:

1. Preheat the air fryer to 350°F .

2. Whisk the sugar and melted butter in a medium bowl until well combined. Whisk in the egg substitute or egg , then the sour cream and vanilla until smooth. Remove the whisk and stir in the flour, baking powder, and salt with a wooden spoon just until a soft dough forms.

3. Use 2 tablespoons of this dough to create a ball between your clean palms. Set it aside and continue making balls: 8 more for the small batch, 12 more for the medium batch, or 17 more for the large one.

4. Coat the balls in the vegetable oil spray, then set them in the basket with as much air space between them as possible. Even a fraction of an inch will be enough, but they should not touch. Air-fry undisturbed for 12 minutes, or until browned and cooked through. A toothpick inserted into the center of a ball should come out clean.

5. Pour the contents of the basket onto a wire rack. Cool for at least 5 minutes before serving.

Chewy Coconut Cake

Servings: 6

Cooking Time: 18-22 Minutes

Ingredients:

- ¾ cup plus 2½ tablespoons All-purpose flour
- ¾ teaspoon Baking powder
- ⅛ teaspoon Table salt
- 7½ tablespoons (1 stick minus ½ tablespoon) Butter, at room temperature
- ⅓ cup plus 1 tablespoon Granulated white sugar
- 5 tablespoons Packed light brown sugar
- 5 tablespoons Pasteurized egg substitute, such as Egg Beaters
- 2 teaspoons Vanilla extract
- ½ cup Unsweetened shredded coconut (see here)
- Baking spray

Directions:

1. Preheat the air fryer to 325°F (or 330°F, if that's the closest setting).

2. Mix the flour, baking powder, and salt in a small bowl until well combined.

3. Using an electric hand mixer at medium speed , beat the butter, granulated white sugar, and brown sugar in a medium bowl until creamy and smooth, about 3 minutes, occasionally scraping down the inside of the bowl. Beat in the egg substitute or egg and vanilla until smooth.

4. Scrape down and remove the beaters. Fold in the flour mixture with a rubber spatula just until all the flour is moistened. Fold in the coconut until the mixture is a uniform color.

5. Use the baking spray to generously coat the inside of a 6-inch round cake pan for a small batch, a 7-inch round cake pan for a medium batch, or an 8-inch round cake pan for a large batch. Scrape and spread the batter into the pan, smoothing the batter out to an even layer.

6. Set the pan in the basket and air-fry for 18 minutes for a 6-inch layer, 20 minutes for a 7-inch layer, or 22 minutes for an 8-inch layer, or until the cake is well browned and set even if there's a little soft give right at the center. Start checking it at the 16-minute mark to know where you are.

7. Use hot pads or silicone baking mitts to transfer the cake pan to a wire rack. Cool for at least 1 hour or up to 4 hours. Use a nonstick-safe knife to slice the cake into wedges right in the pan, lifting them out one by one.

Coconut-carrot Cupcakes

Servings: 4
Cooking Time: 25 Minutes
Ingredients:

- 1 cup flour
- ½ tsp baking soda
- 1/3 cup light brown sugar
- ¼ tsp salt
- ¼ tsp ground cinnamon
- 1 ½ tsp vanilla extract
- 1 egg
- 1 tbsp buttermilk
- 1 tbsp vegetable oil
- ¼ cup grated carrots
- 2 tbsp coconut shreds
- 6 oz cream cheese
- 1 1/3 cups powdered sugar
- 2 tbsp butter, softened
- 1 tbsp milk
- 1 tbsp coconut flakes

Directions:

1. Preheat air fryer at 375ºF. Combine flour, baking soda, brown sugar, salt, and cinnamon in a bowl. In another bowl, combine egg, 1 tsp of vanilla, buttermilk, and vegetable oil. Pour wet ingredients into dry ingredients and toss to combine. Do not overmix. Fold in carrots and coconut shreds. Spoon mixture into 8 greased silicone cupcake liners. Place cupcakes in the frying basket and Bake for 6-8 minutes. Let cool onto a cooling rack for 15 minutes. Whisk cream cheese, powdered sugar, remaining vanilla, softened butter, and milk in a bowl until smooth. Spread over cooled cupcakes. Garnish with coconut flakes and serve.

Fried Oreos

Servings: 12
Cooking Time: 6 Minutes Per Batch
Ingredients:

- oil for misting or nonstick spray
- 1 cup complete pancake and waffle mix
- 1 teaspoon vanilla extract
- ½ cup water, plus 2 tablespoons
- 12 Oreos or other chocolate sandwich cookies
- 1 tablespoon confectioners' sugar

Directions:

1. Spray baking pan with oil or nonstick spray and place in basket.
2. Preheat air fryer to 390°F.
3. In a medium bowl, mix together the pancake mix, vanilla, and water.
4. Dip 4 cookies in batter and place in baking pan.
5. Cook for 6minutes, until browned.
6. Repeat steps 4 and 5 for the remaining cookies.
7. Sift sugar over warm cookies.

Custard

Servings: 4
Cooking Time: 45 Minutes

Ingredients:

- 2 cups whole milk
- 2 eggs
- ¼ cup sugar
- ⅛ teaspoon salt
- ¼ teaspoon vanilla
- cooking spray
- ⅛ teaspoon nutmeg

Directions:

1. In a blender, process milk, egg, sugar, salt, and vanilla until smooth.
2. Spray a 6 x 6-inch baking pan with nonstick spray and pour the custard into it.
3. Cook at 300°F for 45 minutes. Custard is done when the center sets.
4. Sprinkle top with the nutmeg.
5. Allow custard to cool slightly.
6. Serve it warm, at room temperature, or chilled.

Mini Carrot Cakes

Servings: 6
Cooking Time: 25 Minutes

Ingredients:

- 1 cup grated carrots
- ¼ cup raw honey
- ¼ cup olive oil
- ½ tsp vanilla extract
- ½ tsp lemon zest
- 1 egg
- ¼ cup applesauce
- 1 1/3 cups flour
- ¾ tsp baking powder
- ½ tsp baking soda
- ½ tsp ground cinnamon
- ¼ tsp ground nutmeg
- ⅛ tsp ground ginger
- ⅛ tsp salt
- ¼ cup chopped hazelnuts
- 2 tbsp chopped sultanas

Directions:

1. Preheat air fryer to 380°F. Combine the carrots, honey, olive oil, vanilla extract, lemon zest, egg, and applesauce in a bowl. Sift the flour, baking powder, baking soda, cinnamon, nutmeg, ginger, and salt in a separate bowl. Add the wet ingredients to the dry ingredients, mixing until just combined. Fold in the hazelnuts and sultanas. Fill greased muffin cups three-quarters full with the batter, and place them in the frying basket. Bake for 10-12 minutes until a toothpick inserted in the center of a cupcake comes out clean. Serve and enjoy!

Spanish Churro Bites

Servings: 5
Cooking Time: 35 Minutes
Ingredients:

- ¼ tsp salt
- 2 tbsp vegetable oil
- 3 tbsp white sugar
- 1 cup flour
- ½ tsp ground cinnamon
- 2 tbsp granulated sugar

Directions:

1. On the stovetop, add 1 cup of water, salt, 1 tbsp of vegetable oil and 1 tbsp sugar in a pot. Bring to a boil over high heat. Remove from the heat and add flour. Stir with a wooden spoon until the flour is combined and a ball of dough forms. Cool for 5 minutes. Put the ball of dough in a plastic pastry bag with a star tip. Squeeze the dough to the tip and twist the top of the bag. Squeeze 10 strips of dough, about 5-inches long each, onto a workspace. Spray with cooking oil.

2. Preheat air fryer to 340°F. Place the churros in the greased frying basket and Air Fry for 22-25 minutes, flipping once halfway through until golden. Meanwhile, heat the remaining vegetable oil in a small bowl. In another shallow bowl, mix the remaining 2 tbsp sugar and cinnamon. Roll the cooked churros in cinnamon sugar. Top with granulated sugar and serve immediately.

Rustic Berry Layer Cake

Servings: 6
Cooking Time: 45 Minutes
Ingredients:

- 2 eggs, beaten
- ½ cup milk
- 2 tbsp Greek yogurt
- ¼ cup maple syrup
- 1 tbsp apple cider vinegar
- 1 tbsp vanilla extract
- ¾ cup all-purpose flour
- 1 tsp baking powder
- ½ tsp baking soda
- ¼ cup dark chocolate chips
- 1/3 cup raspberry jam

Directions:

1. Preheat air fryer to 350°F. Combine the eggs, milk, Greek yogurt, maple syrup, apple vinegar, and vanilla extract in a bowl. Toss in flour, baking powder, and baking soda until combined. Pour the batter into a 6-inch round cake pan, distributing well, and Bake for 20-25 minutes until a toothpick comes out clean. Let cool completely.

2. Turn the cake onto a plate, cut lengthwise to make 2 equal layers. Set aside. Add chocolate chips to a heat-proof bowl and Bake for 3 minutes until fully melted. In the meantime, spread raspberry jam on top of the bottom layer, distributing well, and top with the remaining layer. Once the chocolate is ready, stir in 1 tbsp of milk. Pour over the layer cake and spread well. Cut into 6 wedges and serve immediately.

Cherry Cheesecake Rolls

Servings: 6
Cooking Time: 30 Minutes

Ingredients:

- 1 can crescent rolls
- 4 oz cream cheese
- 1 tbsp cherry preserves
- 1/3 cup sliced fresh cherries

Directions:

1. Roll out the dough into a large rectangle on a flat work surface. Cut the dough into 12 rectangles by cutting 3 cuts across and 2 cuts down. In a microwave-safe bowl, soften cream cheese for 15 seconds. Stir together with cherry preserves. Mound 2 tsp of the cherries-cheese mix on each piece of dough. Carefully spread the mixture but not on the edges. Top with 2 tsp of cherries each. Roll each triangle to make a cylinder.

2. Preheat air fryer to 350°F. Place the first batch of the rolls in the greased air fryer. Spray the rolls with cooking oil and Bake for 8 minutes. Let cool in the air fryer for 2-3 minutes before removing. Serve.

Apple Dumplings

Servings: 4
Cooking Time: 25 Minutes

Ingredients:

- 1 Basic Pie Dough (see the following recipe)
- 4 medium Granny Smith or Pink Lady apples, peeled and cored
- 4 tablespoons sugar
- 4 teaspoons cinnamon
- ½ teaspoon ground nutmeg
- 4 tablespoons unsalted butter, melted
- 4 scoops ice cream, for serving

Directions:

1. Preheat the air fryer to 330°F.

2. Bring the pie crust recipe to room temperature.

3. Place the pie crust on a floured surface. Divide the dough into 4 equal pieces. Roll out each piece to ¼-inch-thick rounds. Place an apple onto each dough round. Sprinkle 1 tablespoon of sugar in the core part of each apple; sprinkle 1 teaspoon cinnamon and ⅛ teaspoon nutmeg over each. Place 1 tablespoon of butter into the center of each. Fold up the sides and fully cover the cored apples.

4. Place the dumplings into the air fryer basket and spray with cooking spray. Cook for 25 minutes. Check after 14 minutes cooking; if they're getting too brown, reduce the heat to 320°F and complete the cooking.

5. Serve hot apple dumplings with a scoop of ice cream.

Sweet Potato Donut Holes

Servings: 18
Cooking Time: 4 Minutes Per Batch

Ingredients:

- 1 cup flour
- ⅓ cup sugar
- ¼ teaspoon baking soda
- 1 teaspoon baking powder
- ⅛ teaspoon salt
- ½ cup cooked mashed purple sweet potatoes
- 1 egg, beaten
- 2 tablespoons butter, melted
- 1 teaspoon pure vanilla extract
- oil for misting or cooking spray

Directions:

1. Preheat air fryer to 390°F.
2. In a large bowl, stir together the flour, sugar, baking soda, baking powder, and salt.
3. In a separate bowl, combine the potatoes, egg, butter, and vanilla and mix well.
4. Add potato mixture to dry ingredients and stir into a soft dough.
5. Shape dough into 1½-inch balls. Mist lightly with oil or cooking spray.
6. Place 9 donut holes in air fryer basket, leaving a little space in between. Cook for 4 minutes, until done in center and lightly browned outside.
7. Repeat step 6 to cook remaining donut holes.

Pecan-oat Filled Apples

Servings: 4
Cooking Time: 20 Minutes

Ingredients:

- 2 cored Granny Smith apples, halved
- ¼ cup rolled oats
- 2 tbsp honey
- ½ tsp ground cinnamon
- ½ tsp ground ginger
- 2 tbsp chopped pecans
- A pinch of salt
- 1 tbsp olive oil

Directions:

1. Preheat air fryer to 380°F. Combine together the oats, honey, cinnamon, ginger, pecans, salt, and olive oil in a bowl. Scoop a quarter of the oat mixture onto the top of each half apple. Put the apples in the frying basket and Roast for 12-15 minutes until the apples are fork-tender.

Carrot Cake With Cream Cheese Icing

Servings: 6
Cooking Time: 55 Minutes

Ingredients:

- 1¼ cups all-purpose flour
- 1 teaspoon baking powder
- ½ teaspoon baking soda
- 1 teaspoon ground cinnamon
- ¼ teaspoon ground nutmeg
- ¼ teaspoon salt
- 2 cups grated carrot (about 3 to 4 medium carrots or 2 large)
- ¾ cup granulated sugar
- ¼ cup brown sugar
- 2 eggs
- ¾ cup canola or vegetable oil
- For the icing:
- 8 ounces cream cheese, softened at room , Temperature: 8 tablespoons butter (4 ounces or 1 stick), softened at room , Temperature: 1 cup powdered sugar
- 1 teaspoon pure vanilla extract

Directions:

1. Grease a 7-inch cake pan.

2. Combine the flour, baking powder, baking soda, cinnamon, nutmeg and salt in a bowl. Add the grated carrots and toss well. In a separate bowl, beat the sugars and eggs together until light and frothy. Drizzle in the oil, beating constantly. Fold the egg mixture into the dry ingredients until everything is just combined and you no longer see any traces of flour. Pour the batter into the cake pan and wrap the pan completely in greased aluminum foil.

3. Preheat the air fryer to 350°F.

4. Lower the cake pan into the air fryer basket using a sling made of aluminum foil (fold a piece of aluminum foil into a strip about 2-inches wide by 24-inches long). Fold the ends of the aluminum foil into the air fryer, letting them rest on top of the cake. Air-fry for 40 minutes. Remove the aluminum foil cover and air-fry for an additional 15 minutes or until a skewer inserted into the center of the cake comes out clean and the top is nicely browned.

5. While the cake is cooking, beat the cream cheese, butter, powdered sugar and vanilla extract together using a hand mixer, stand mixer or food processor (or a lot of elbow grease!).

6. Remove the cake pan from the air fryer and let the cake cool in the cake pan for 10 minutes or so. Then remove the cake from the pan and let it continue to cool completely. Frost the cake with the cream cheese icing and serve.

Printed in Great Britain
by Amazon